ASSAM VALLEY

AHOM GIRL.

[Frontispiece.

ASSAM VALLEY

Beliefs and Customs of the Assamese Hindus

By

R. C. MUIRHEAD THOMSON, D.Sc.

LONDON

LUZAC & COMPANY LTD.

1948

88380

Printed in Great Britain
at the BURLEIGH PRESS, *Lewins Mead,* BRISTOL

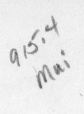

CONTENTS

LIST OF ILLUSTRATIONS

FOREWORD

In these days when the number of books on travel and foreign countries is increasing year by year, I feel that some sort of explanation is due as to why this book was written.

The man who travels in the East is soon aware that some countries are more fully described than others, and that there are numerous books written about some parts of the East, and very few about others. For example, the visitor to Ceylon, Burma, or Malaya will find, if he is interested, an attractive assortment of books dealing with these lands and the people who live there. And he will have little difficulty in acquiring, by reading alone, a general idea of the people and their customs, and a solid background into which he can fit his own observations and experiences. Once this knowledge has been gained, the more advanced books and anthropological monographs appear much less formidable than before. Those who become really interested in the lives of the people round them find every encouragement to put their own observations on a sounder and more scientific basis.

The person who is going to spend any time in Assam, on the other hand, finds himself in a much less fortunate position. This small corner of India is a meeting place of so many races and customs that it has long been recognised by the anthropologist as one of the most productive fields for research work. As a result, no area of such a limited size can boast of such an impressive array of monographs ; one can find over a dozen classical studies dealing with the various Naga tribes, with the Meitheis, the Khasis, the Garos, and so on. But practically all these works deal with tribes inhabiting the hills round Assam, primitive people with tribal culture and belief.

The great plains, however, forming the valley of the Brahmaputra or the Assam valley, have received scant

attention. It is to this valley that the bulk of the Assamese
speaking people are confined, and, with the exception of
the single hill state of Manipur, Hinduism also is confined
to the plains. The great tea garden industry is also limited
to the Brahmaputra and Surma valleys ; cultivation, unlike
that of Ceylon or Darjeeling, stopping at the foothills.
The bulk of the Europeans associated directly or indirectly
with tea planting, spend the greater part of their lives in
the valley, and not in the hills.

The people of the valley are so sharply marked off from
the hill tribes that these full and detailed monographs
described above give one little or no idea about life and
customs in the plains. Some of the non-Hindu tribes who
have settled in different parts of the valley have been described in *The Kacharis* by the Rev. S. Endle, and there is
much interesting material in Gurdon's *Some Assamese,
Proverbs*. Gait's *History of Assam* is an indispensible mine
of information on all matters historical, though naturally
it does not concern itself so much with present day con-
ditions. There is useful but scattered information in the
Census reports ; and there have been a few books describing the life of the tea planter from the European point of
view. With the exception of these, and of a few brief
papers scattered through the annals of learned societies,
and not easily accessible to the ordinary reader, there is
practically nothing to introduce the visitor to the people
and customs of the Assam valley.

During the three and a half years I spent in Assam I
found this lack of guidance a grave handicap. The significance of so much that I saw remained obscure for too long,
and in many ways, particularly with regard to religious
background, I learnt more after I had left Assam than
when I was actually there. During that period I was
engaged in work of an entirely different nature, and all the
observations contained in this book were spare time studies
accumulated when there was time and when the spirit
moved me. In this last clause the movement of the spirit
is a much more potent factor than the lack of time. In the

sultry enervating climate of Assam enthusiasm tends to wane and interest to flag ; and after leaving the country one is amazed and horrified to look back on the simple things left undone, the ragged ends, the obvious opportunities missed, and the peculiar mental laziness, or ' Assam rot ' that may overtake one after three or four rainy seasons.

One is also faced with the fact that many Hindus, even educated ones, are not very helpful at describing their own customs and beliefs, and that their opinions in turn are mainly determined by their caste and social position. In approaching a study of life in Assam I have found that some knowledge of Hindu mythology is a most valuable asset, and that a familiarity with the numerous Hindu deities and heroes, and with the great epics such as the Ramayana and Mahabharata, strikes a common chord even with the illiterate villager. When we remember that with Hinduism there is no clear distinction between mythology and religion, and that religion in turn may determine the whole mode of life and every day actions of the people, the chain of reasoning must be obvious.

Those who are much more familiar with Assam and the Assamese than I am will doubtless find much to criticise in this book ; much that is superficial ; many curious gaps in knowledge, and possibly mistakes and misrepresentations. But I have tried, mainly from my own observations, to write the kind of book which I myself would have appreciated on my first introduction to the Assamese Hindus ; and it is to be hoped that others too may find something here to stimulate their interest in the people and their customs.

CHAPTER I

INTRODUCTION TO THE ASSAMESE

THE province of Assam is divided into three fairly distinct regions. The Hills; the Surma Valley; and the Assam Valley or Valley of the Brahmaputra. The Hills are occupied by numerous primitive non-hindu tribes such as Nagas, Abors, Kukis, Miris, etc., which do not concern us here. The Surma Valley is in many ways more allied to Bengal than to Assam, and the majority of its people are Mohammedans. The Assam or Brahmaputra Valley is where the bulk of the Assamese-speaking people live, and where Hinduism is predominant; and it is to this valley that our observations are confined.

Besides the Assamese, there are numerous groups of aboriginal tribes in different parts of the valley, such as Chutiya, Miri, Lalung, Kachari, Mech and so on. Although many of them have been living in the valley for centuries there are still large numbers who are tribal and animistic in belief. Others have adopted some Hindu practices while keeping up the old tribal customs, and there are others again who consider themselves true Hindus.

Considering how long all the people of the valley have been in contact with Hindu ideas, it is surprising how the tribal beliefs have persisted. One can find in the Valley all gradations from orthodox Hindu to complete tribalism with no trace of Hindu beliefs. It is this indefinite borderline between Hindus and non-Hindus, and also the fact that the position changes from year to year, which has proved a constant source of dissention and dissatisfaction among those who supervise the 10-yearly cenus of the province. In the censuses of 1921 and 1931 there were good reasons for believing that many people belonging to these backward tribes mentioned above had returned their religion as Hindu, either in the belief that it gave them a stamp of respectability, or under the persuasion of the biassed Hindu enumerator. Furthermore the activities of the Hindu mission, or Hindu Sabha of Assam, were directed towards persuading backward tribesmen that they really were Hindus. The Mikirs for example, tribal people inhabiting the low Mikir hills in the centre of the valley, were told that they were descended from Bali Rajah, and were therefore really Hindus of ancient lineage; an argument for conversion, by the way, which was used with such success by the Brahmins, centuries before, in their attempts to convert the Ahom and Kachari rulers of Assam.

Altogether, apart from the well-established Hindu castes in Assam, it is impossible to form even a rough estimate of the extent of Hinduism in Assam. The compilers of the most recent—1941—census have decided to make tribe, and not religion, the basis of classification. As a result the 1941 census shows an apparent decrease of about 600,000 Hindus compared with 1931, while the number of tribals has apparently increased by over a quarter of a million in the same period. It is obvious that the position is not yet cleared up satisfactorily.

Of the numerous castes or groups of Hindus in Assam valley we need only dwell on a few of the more outstanding.

The Brahmins, who form the highest or priestly caste number about 110,000 in the valley (1931 figures). They are descendents of the numerous Brahmins brought into Assam from other parts of India, particularly during the time of the Ahom Kings who ruled in Assam from the 13th to the 19th century. In the course of centuries they have absorbed into their blood enough of the Mongoloid element to make them differ little in general appearance from other high caste Assamese. The original Brahmins were introduced, not from the neighbouring province of Bengal, but from further west, and there is a closer affinity between the Brahmins of Assam and those of United Provinces and Orissa, than with those of Bengal. The Brahmins are the only caste who have the privilege of becoming priests, but apart from that one can find them in practically all occupations from clerk to lawyer, doctor, or District Commissioner. A characteristic Brahmin name, not found in any other caste, is Goswami.

Between the Brahmins and the rest of the Hindus come the Kayasthas—about 40,000 in the Assam Valley, who are closely allied to the Brahmins, but have not the privilege of becoming priests. A characteristic name is Dutta.

To the Assamese Brahmins, all non-Brahmins are called Sudras, a term which in India is usually restricted to the lowest or serf caste.

One of the largest groups of non-Brahmins is the Kalita (Kolita) caste, which together with the Ahoms contains most of the well-established orthodox Hindus. Although the Kalitas remain fairly distinct, their origin is still a matter of conjecture. They are usually supposed to be the descendents of the first Aryan immigrants into Assam by women of the country. While many of them are indistinguishable in appearance from the typical Mongoloid Assamese, others have a distinctly Aryan cast of countenance, resembling that of the classical Hindu type. There are supposed to be about 300,000 Kalitas in the Assam Valley. Allied to the Kalitas are the Keots and Hindu Koch (Kos).

The next main division, caste, or tribe, the Ahoms, is a particularly interesting one. Most of the present day Ahoms are descended from the Ahom kings and their ruling families. The Ahoms originally invaded Assam from the Upper Shan States in Burma, and in the course of a few hundred years made themselves complete masters of the Assam Valley. They overthrew the powerful Chutiya, Kachari and Koch rajahs who had been firmly established in Assam for centuries, and were even strong enough to stop the hitherto irresistable Mohammedan invaders who had swept victoriously right across North India.

The present day Ahoms occupy a peculiar position in the Hindu scale. Although the majority of them are well established Hindus, very like the Kalitas, yet as a tribe they remain so distinct that the ordinary Assamese still talks about ' Hindus and Ahoms ' as two separate groups. Most Assamese who claim to be Ahoms only do so when they are fairly certain that they are of noble ancestry. The lower class Ahoms prefer to be called Kalitas.

The Ahoms are entirely confined to the Assam valley, and mostly to Upper Assam in Sibsagar subdivision, and there are probably about a quarter of a million of them all told.

These castes between them make up from a quarter to a third of the $3\frac{1}{2}$ million Hindus in the Assam valley. Of the remainder the bulk are tea-garden coolies imported from outside Assam. They are not Assamese and do not concern us here. The rest is made up of hinduised Chutiyas, Kacharis, and so on. Many of these are ill-defined Hindus, and exhibit every gradation and variation of belief.

An interesting group of people on the borderline of conversion are the Chaudangs, descendents of the body-guard and executioners of the Ahom kings. In an old description of Assam the author says "A bodyguard of six or seven thousand Asamians, fierce as demons, of unshaken courage, and well provided with warlike arms and accoutre-ments always keep watch near the Rajah's sitting and sleeping apartments ; these are his loyal and confidential troops and patrol ". The present day Chaudangs are mainly restricted to the neighbourhood of Sibsagar and Jorhat, old headquarters of the Assamese kings. Many of the Chaudangs remain outside the fold of Hinduism as lao-pani drinkers and eaters of pigs' flesh, but some of the more wealthy ones attempt to better themselves in the social scale either by calling themselves Ahoms or Kalitas, taking names for themselves such as Phukan or Barua originally indicative of distinguished position, or by adopting certain Hindu customs, such as holding proper marriage ceremonies with a priest officiating.

Allied to the Chaudangs are the Tengals and the Hunwals, the latter of whom were originally the caste who specialised in washing river sand for gold under the Ahom kings.

Of the large group of ' Hindu exterior castes ' the most

JOYSAGAR TANK AND TEMPLE

TANK OVERGROWN WITH WATER LILIES, WHERE RUDRA SINGH IS SAID
TO HAVE WASHED HIS SWORD AFTER A BATTLE.

[To face page 16]

AHOM GIRL.

conspicuous are the Doms, or as they prefer to be known as, the Kaibortas. These are low caste Assamese, possibly of Dravidian origin. One commonly sees groups of Dom women and girls netting fish in the swamps and bheels alongside the main roads. Many of them wear these enormously broad-brimmed Shan hats. As the Doms are rather coarse in speech and features, and as they are so conspicuous on the roads, the visitor is apt to form a poor opinion of the Assamese country people, thinking that they are typical of the Assamese. The Doms or Kaibortas are very low in the social scale, not because they catch fish, but because there is a stigma attached to the selling of fish, their main occupation.

Each of the main castes, such as Brahmin, Kayastha, Kalita and Ahom, remain fairly distinct, but mixed marriages occasionally take place. Although it is strongly discouraged, a Brahmin boy may marry a Sudra (non-Brahmin) girl, cutting himself off from his own Brahmin relations. Recently an inter-provincial marriage between a Brahmin boy and a Kalita girl was attended by distinguished guests, and there is not necessarily any slur or scandal attached to such a match. There are also occasional matches between high class Kalitas and high class Ahoms, but, in general, it is remarkable how distinct these castes remain in Assam, where they are so closely allied and must have a great deal of common ancestry.

The beliefs and customs of the high caste Assamese Hindus have a great deal in common, but at the same time there are other practices, which appear to be limited to one caste or even to a section of that caste. A Brahmin, for example, may disclaim any knowledge of customs peculiar to the Ahom, and they in turn may profess ignorance of some of the recognized priestly rites. It is not, therefore, easy to generalize about the Assamese, because the term, even when restricted to the inhabitants of the Assam valley or to the Assamese speaking people, really includes many different sects of people with widely different ideas of what Hinduism means.

In this book there is no attempt to describe any esoteric Hindu beliefs, or any of the philosophies of Hinduism. No doubt many of the Brahmins are familiar with the more profound and intellectual side of their religion, but I think that to the average Assamese Hinduism means popular Hinduism; the personalities, lives and deeds of the main Hindu deities, and their various incarnations on earth; the classic stories from the Puranas, the Ramayana and the Mahabharata; and also the numerous Hindu customs which affect their daily lives, and the rules of conduct laid down in the Shastras. Anything more philosophical, such as the meaning of ' world soul ', ' absolute being ', ' world substance ', or ' elemental soul ' is probably as unintelligible to them as it is to me.

Of all the various Hindu deities, most prominence is commonly given to the great triad of gods, Brahma ' the creator ', Vishnu ' the preserver ', and Siva ' the destroyer '. In actual practice this gives rather a misleading conception of their functions and importance, because the vast majority of Hindus are followers of either Vishnu or of Siva.

Vishnu has appeared on earth in various forms or avatars. One of these was as Rama, the great hero of the Ramayana; another one was as Krishna.

The popular conception of Krishna is as a boy, the cowherd, round whom endless tales have accumulated as to his boyish pranks, his light hearted dallying with the Gopis, or milkmaids, his passionate love for Radha, and his great prowess in frustrating the evil designs of giants and monsters. All these tales are well known to the Assamese, and his name is invoked in numerous love songs and wedding songs.

The other aspect of Krishna is when he appears in a more mature form in the Mahabharata, and delivers his divine message and gospel as the Bhagavad Gita.

The birth anniversary of Lord Sri Krishna is celebrated as Janmastami all over Assam, and is the occasion of learned discourses by distinguished Assamese expounding the doctrine and teaching of Krishna. The more frolicsome and boyish aspect of Krishna is celebrated in another annual festival known as Doljatra, Fagua, or Holi ; the occasion of much boistrous behaviour, and the squirting of red coloured water from bamboo syringes over the passers-by.

All Assamese Hindus celebrate these festivals and acknowledge Krishna ; but one sect—the Mahapurushias —deify him to the exclusion of all others, and they will be discussed separately.

The other deity, Siva, is of particular interest in Assam, not only on his own account, but because of the adoration given to his female aspect, consort, or counterpart in her various forms known as Durga, Parvati, Kali, and so on. A fuller account of these deities is given in the following pages.

CHAPTER II

SIVA

To millions of Hindus in India Siva is the great god, the Maha-deva, compared with whom all other deities are insignificant. He, by himself, is capable of creating, preserving, and destroying ; he is the bestower of blessings, and has all the attributes necessary to hold the undivided attention and adoration of his worshippers.

As the Lord of Mountains he has his abode in Himalaya. Siva did not always hold this position of authority he now has. There is no mention of him in the oldest Hindu scriptures, and when he does appear for the first time it is not in his full blaze of glory. Only by asceticism and rigorous austerities has he reached his present state, and he is therefore usually pictured as the Divine Yogi, sitting cross-legged in meditation, his light reddish hair coiled and matted ; clothed only in a tiger skin, his naked body is pale with the dust of ashes ; his throat dark blue with a snake coiled round or garlanded with skulls of men. In one hand he holds his characteristic weapon, the trident, and with the other he makes the gesture that bestows blessings. By his very simplicity Siva stands apart from the other gods with their many possessions. In his Yogi position his trident may be replaced by a wooden staff and an axe.

In accordance with his numerous attributes Siva has a host of names. Some of them derive from incidents in his life, others from his different aspects and activities. One could fill a book with a mere selection of all his names and the stories built round them. For the present it would serve no useful purpose to catalogue them here, but it is as well to remember that many of his other names are actually used by worshippers, and in hymns of praise.

The followers of Siva, the Sivaites, exalt him above all other gods, and describe incidents from the sacred books to show that even Brahma and Vishnu are humbled in his presence.

One of the great Hindu epics, the Ramayana, is concerned with Ravanna, the 10-headed, 20-armed demon king of Ceylon. Despite his evil nature Ravanna was able, by means of incredible austerities and penances, to build up such reserves of power as to threaten the gods themselves. Finally Vishnu was sent down to earth in the form of the great hero, Rama, with the express purpose of removing this threat to divine power. He eventually managed to do this, but only after gigantic battles, and with the help of vast armies and divine weapons. Early in his life Ravanna used to go every day to Mount Kailasa, the Himalayan abode of Siva. He got weary of this after a time and decided it would be simpler to remove Kailasa bodily to Ceylon. When he started to pull up the mountain, the trembling earth frightened Siva's wife. Siva, roused from meditation, merely moved his toe and sent the mighty Ravanna tumbling through space to the nether regions. Such was the power of Siva that he could dispatch with a gesture a demon powerful enough to threaten the existence of Vishnu himself.

On a different occasion the gods decided that another demon who was becoming embarassingly powerful could best be destroyed by a son who would be born to Siva and his wife Parvati. In order to rouse the necessary passion in Siva, and make him unite with his wife, Kama, the god of Love, his consort, Rati (Desire), and his companion, the Spring (Vasanta), proceeded to Mount Kailasa. This combination of deities was usually so powerful that the gods themselves gave way to passion under their influence. Siva was given up to Yogi meditation when Kama shot his arrow at him, but so great was the power and self-control of Siva, that he was moved only to anger at being disturbed, and with a flash of fire from his third eye he consumed Kama to ashes.

Another story tells how some demons (Rakshasas) had stored up great merit by worshipping Brahma, and finally were in a position to ask Brahma for power to destroy the whole world. Brahma's half-consent alarmed the other gods, and they called in Siva to save the world. This he did by dancing his mighty dance, the Tandavan, to distract Brahma ; a dance so mighty that it threatened the existence of the world and almost defeated its own ends. This is a very popular incident with Hindu dancers, and is frequently acted by the troupes of players who tour Assam from time to time.

The followers of Siva also tell how Vishnu himself was wont to worship Siva daily with a thousand lotuses. Such was his devotion that one day when he found one lotus missing, he plucked out his own eye rather than break the continuity of his worship.

In one well-known hymn extolling the greatness of Siva, the author sums up in the following words :—

> " Oh Lord, if the Giver of Happiness were to write
>   for all time,
> With a pen made from the branch of the best of all
>   celestial trees.
> Using the whole earth as her leaf
> With a black mass of ink,
> As wide as the great ocean,
> Still would it be impossible to express the fullness
>   of thy attributes."

Most of the Hindu gods and goddesses are commonly represented by images and sculptures, but it is only in South India that Siva is represented in this way, and nearly always as the Dancing Siva—Siva Nataraja. By far the most widespread form or emblem of Siva, and practically the only one in Assam, is the *linga* or male organ. This usually takes the form of a cylindrical stone pillar—the linga—set upright on a flat circular base, the gauri patta, which represents the female organ or yoni of the goddess (gauri).

It is as well at this stage to point out that the Westerner must not take too literal a view of these objects. To him, with his peculiar upbringing and prejudices, they have a significance entirely different to that of the Hindu worshipper. To most Hindus it has no phallic significance as we understand it, and most of them would be surprised and shocked by the reactions of the average European on first learning the meaning of these emblems. (Even the Abbé Dubois, one of the pioneer students of Indian customs, and whose book on *Hindu manners, customs and ceremonies* has been a classic for over a century, was compelled to write as follows : ' It is incredible, it is impossible to believe that in inventing this vile superstition the religious teachers of India intended that the people should render direct worship to objects the very names of which, among civilized nations, are an insult to decency '.)

A highly intelligent Hindu friend of mine told me that although he had been familiar with the linga from childhood, it was only when he was a young man that he found out about its origin from Siva's male organ ; and his sudden awareness was probably not unaffected by his contact with western ideas and culture.

If we could approach the subject dispassionately, the association of sex organs with religion—an idea abhorrent to western minds—appears as logical and realistic as many other Hindu ideas. Death and dissolution are represented by the grave and the cremation ground ; and in the same way conception and creation are represented by the coming together of male and female, and the union of the essential organs. We shall have more to say about this aspect of Hinduism when discussing the Saktas.

How important the linga is may be gathered from the scriptures, one of which, the Mahanirvana Tantra says " There is no doubt that by the installation of a Shiva linga a man acquires ten million times the merit which is acquired by giving the world and all its gold, by the performance of ten thousand horse sacrifices, by the digging of a tank in a waterless country, or by making happy the poor or such as are enfeebled by disease ".

And again " The land within a radius of a hundred cubits

of the linga is declared to be Siva-kshetra " (i.e. holy land of Siva).

In the same scripture mentioned above several pages are devoted to detailed instructions about worshipping Siva in the form of his linga ; in which the linga is washed and bathed frequently, adorned with garlands of sweet-smelling flowers, all to the accompaniment of appropriate gestures, prayers and incantations.

One of the temples near Sibsagar in Upper Assam (a town, incidentally, which takes its name from Siva) has a great stone linga, three or four feet long, which can be set into the hollow of a great boulder, as the gauri patta. In that part of the country there are no stones in the alluvial soil, and the boulder is said to have been brought from the banks of the Dikhu River emerging from the foothills many miles away.

Another famous Assam linga is the great bana-linga in the Siva temple of Neghereting near the Brahmaputra. It is about three feet high and the same in breadth, and was discovered over three hundred years ago during the reign of the Ahom Rajah, Pratap Singh.

In the temple ruins at Tezpore there is a brick shrine containing a linga seven feet in girth, in a circular yoni seven to eight feet in diameter, as well as several other lingas fitted into yonis.

The name of Siva is familiar to all Assamese Hindus, even in the most remote villages ; he is also commonly known under another name, Hodakia. Siva is reported to have over a thousand names, of which thirty or forty are the most common alternatives, but Hodakia, peculiar to Assam, is not one of these. Possibly, by a familiar process in the Assamese language, in which the s at the beginning of a Bengali or Sanskrit word is turned into h, it may be derived from Sadhaka and signify the Divine Worshipper or Yogi.

Siva's consort is Parvati, who is known by many other different forms, such as Durga, Kali, Uma, and Devi the goddess. They are considered inseparable and essential to each other, the male and female aspects of one unity. The goddess, however, achieves in North-East India and Assam an importance unknown elsewhere, and by herself is the object of worship and adoration by millions of Assamese.

CHAPTER III

DURGA

THE worship of Siva's wife, particularly in the form of Durga as a mother-goddess, is one of the most striking features of Hinduism in Bengal and Assam. In her benign aspect, with all the tender appealing womanly traits of a wife and mother, she probably makes a closer appeal to the hearts of her worshippers than any other deity. To the women of Assam particularly she is Debi (Devi the goddess) and Mai (the mother). She, more than any other can offer hope to the young wife praying for a son, and solace to the widow bereft of her husband. In this divine form she is pictured as having all the womanly physical attributes. She has round firm breasts, " untouched save by Mahadeva (Siva) ". A waist so slender that it seems hardly capable of supporting the breasts. A beauteous face with its weight of hanging hair, or " her head with its weight of hair seems covered by a swarm of bees ". Face with large round eyes and noble brow; lips red as the bimba fruit. " Whose form is beauteous as the rising sun, and thy face as that of the full moon ". " The symmetry and smoothness of her thighs are known only to Shiva ", and the beauty of her buttocks have earned her the name Nitambini.

Siva's consort, as we have said before, has many different forms or murtis known by different names. Associated with Siva as the Yogi, the goddess is known as Parvati. Other familiar names besides Durga are Kali, Sati, Uma, Tara, and others. This multiplicity of names is always a bewildering feature of the Hindu mind, and to complicate matters further Durga herself does not always appear in the same aspect or mood. She is also represented as a warlike goddess, a slayer of demons, and saviour of

26

mankind; this is the aspect usually represented in images and sculptures.

The worship of the goddess reaches a peak of fervour in the Durga-puja, one of the happiest and most carefree religious festivals in Assam and Bengal. It falls at that period of the year just after the end of the monsoon rains, corresponding to our month of October. By this time the heavy rain clouds are in retreat, the great floods have passed, and the rivers have returned to their own banks. The rice planting season has finished, and the kett-land is great unbroken sea of tall green rice plants. The hundred and one little country roads are drying up incredibly quickly, and from far and wide crowds of people on foot, on bicycle or bullock cart, converge on the town to see the sacrifice to Durga and the immersion of the goddess in the river.

This festival celebrates two incidents in Durga's life. In her role of benefactor and protector of mankind she is celebrated as the slayer of Mahisasura—a buffalo-headed demon whom she overcomes with the help of her attendant animal, in this case the lion. It is this incident which has given her the name of Mahis-mardini, and which makes the sacrifice of a buffalo a particularly meritorious act to perform at this time.

The festival also celebrates the time when Durga, as a young girl, Uma, is returning home for a few days for the first time after her marriage to the ascetic Lord of Mountains, Siva. It is a great time of the year for family reunions, particularly among the Bengalis, who occupy so many of the positions of clerk or babu in Assam, and who takes the opportunity at this time of returning to their families in Bengal for a few days. It is really the Assamese Christmas time—a season of goodwill and merriment.

In Assam villages, on the first day of the Durga puja, offerings of fruit, vegetables, flowers, etc., and in particular nim trees, are made to the goddess in the village prayer house or namghar. On the following days animals are sacrificed; on one day a white male goat is decapitated, and on another day a male buffalo, representing the demon

Mahis-asura, is sacrificed in a similar way. An hour before the sacrifice the neck of the buffalo is thoroughly massaged with ghee all round till the skin is soft and supple, to facilitate decapitation. The actual sacrifice is made at midday, the animal's legs are tied together, and the animal secured near the image. The head is cut off with one blow of a dao wielded by a Brahmin. Afterwards the buffalo's body may be removed by tea garden coolies, who have no qualms at all about indulging in animal flesh.

The story of Durga and the buffalo-headed demon is familiar to all villagers, and it is recognized that on this day fresh blood is very pleasing to the goddess. The Durga puja culminates in the immersion of the goddess, or rather her image. From early morning the people from the countryside all round have been flocking into town. The buses driven by bearded Punjubis coming in from outlying villages are packed to the doors. Bullock carts covered with a matting hood bring whole families from busti after busti. The roads are thronged with tea garden coolies—foreigners from outside Assam—the women with brightly coloured saris, and arms glistening with cheap gaudy bangles from the bazaar. All the students and babus are there in full strength, wearing spotless white dhotis and loose cotton shirts. At no other time are so many women and girls visible in the streets. Whole family gatherings have assembled along the banks of the river to get an early seat and a good view. All the young girls look delightful in their graceful meghelas (skirts) or saris, even the tiniest chookri (little girl) is dressed like a little woman. With their slim bodies, beautiful glossy black hair parted in the middle, and their solemn little faces, they look entrancing.

The festival attracts plenty of non-Hindus and would-be Hindus too. A troop of Miri girls from the banks of the Brahmaputra have just passed. The lobes of their ears are pierced with thick cylindrical wooden plugs, and they all look around rather self-consciously, feeling strange in the unaccustomed surroundings.

Finally, late in the afternoon, the image of Durga
is carried on the shoulders of a group of college students
through the streets, with a crowd milling behind them.
Durga is represented as the centre figure of a little group.
She is light yellow in colour, wearing a sari and a crown.
Her eight arms are holding various weapons, discus, lance,
axe, shield, arrow, bow and trident, with the last of which
she is giving the death blow to Mahisasura, who is dying
at her feet. She is accompanied by her vahan or attendant
animal, the lion, by her two sons, Ganesh and Kartik,
and by Sarasvati and Lakshmi, wives of Brahma and Vishnu
—but here considered daughters of Durga. With great
rejoicing the whole coloured group in its frame is carried
to the river bank, rowed out to mid-stream, and immersed
in the deep part of the river.

Durga puja seems to be celebrated with fresh enthusiasm
every year, and every year the crowds watch the buffalo
being sacrificed in the temple, and the image immersed in
the river, with the same intense interest as if Mahis-asura
himself was being overcome and destroyed afresh.

The puja, of course, has also its festive and humorous
side. There is always the Indian funny man who makes
a universal appeal with his antics, and who makes the crowd
rock with laughter as his feet slip on the bottom of his
dugout, and he falls theatrically overboard into the river.
The garden coolies too have been spending their wages
on the array of cheap jewellery, bangles, ear-rings, sweet-
meats, and meta-pani (mineral water), temptingly laid out
on booths near the river. They have all been drinking
rice beer (laopani), or sarab (wine) from the shops, and
by nightfall are hilariously and harmlessly drunk. Some
young Chaudang 'lads of the village' who came in with
their girl friends from some busti, have also been indulging.
Their jokes get broader and broader, as they are encouraged
by the titters of their companions, who are also in merry
mood. After a time their remarks become rather indecent,
and there are murmers of disapproval from the respectable
Hindus nearby. Finally a Nepali policeman appears, the

Chaudang becomes truculent, and has to be forcibly removed. Sometimes the squabbles lead to injuries and occasional fatalities. The sweeper, Darwaria, confined by inflexible custom to the sweeper caste, has nevertheless combed his hair carefully, and put on a spotless dhoti, to such effect that he is ruthlessly mocked by his friends, and accused of trying to pass himself off as a clerk.

Finally, long after dark, the last buses and bullock carts have gone ; the last batch of revellers returned to their villages or coolie lines. Silence settles down on the town, and the Durga-puja is over for another year.

CHAPTER IV

KALI

IN the account of Durga we have seen how a goddess, who receives adoration from untold numbers of worshippers is yet depicted as a fierce and ruthless slayer of giants and demons. We are accustomed in the West to the idea of a goddess expressing her goodness to mankind by an appearance of kindness, meekness, or compassion. But here again we have to adjust ourselves to Sakta ideas, which reason that the more terrible and fearsome the aspect of a goddess, the more formidable she will be in vanquishing demons and giants, who threaten the peace and security of her worshippers. As the goddess's main activities in protecting men involve a real blood bath, in which giants are decapitated and devoured, her worshippers evidently consider that they can best show their confidence and adoration by offering her a blood sacrifice.

Along with Durga, the other best known form of Shakti in Assam is Kali, the Black One, who has an even greater propensity for slaughtering and devouring demons than her sister, and whose appearance is correspondingly more fearsome. Kali is usually represented as a black woman with four arms. In one hand she has a sword, in another the head of a giant she has slain, while the other two hands make gestures of encouragement to her worshippers. She wears a long necklace of skulls, and has as her only clothing a girdle of dead men's hands. With her face and breast smeared with blood, and her tongue protruding from her mouth, she dances on the body of her husband —Siva.

All Assamese Hindus are familiar with the story on which this scene is based. Kali, mad with glee, after a particularly decisive victory over the giants, danced with joy till the earth trembled. She was so intoxicated with blood that the only way in which Siva could stop her mad celebration was to lie down among the bodies of the slain. When Kali suddenly caught sight of him under her feet, she thrust out her tongue in shame at the disrespect she had shown to her husband.

Kali, like Durga and all the other Saktis, has innumerable names, which are related to her different attributes. In one well-known hymn to this goddess she is greeted in one hundred different names, all beginning with the letter K ; which gives some indication of the way in which the names of the goddess can be multiplied almost indefinitely.

Kali's outstanding quality is her great liking for blood, and the prominent part played by human sacrifice in her worship. In the famous ' Blood chapter ' of the Kalita Purana full details are given about the animals, whose sacrifice is most pleasing to the goddess. For example, she is said to be pleased for one thousand years by one human sacrifice, and for one hundred thousand years by the sacrifice of three men. In the Blood chapter it is also stated that among those who should not be sacrificed are the female—animal or human—Brahmins, princes, nor 'one who is unwilling'. In many cases the victim must have been a volunteer, who would not only be given certain privileges on earth before his death, but would also gain untold merit by sacrificing himself willingly to Kali. There are numerous records of human sacrifice to Kali in the pages of Assam's history, but it is doubtful if there have been any proved cases in recent times.

The Kali puja is celebrated all over Assam in the autumn, about a month after the Durga puja. It is particularly popular with the tea-garden coolies, who are not indigenous to Assam, but are introduced mainly from Orissa and Chota Nagpur. On that day a black male goat is sacrificed to Kali, whereas all other sacrifices to the goddess are white goats.

The aspect of Kali described above is the one most familiar to the people of Assam ; but besides her usual

ASSAMESE BRAHMIN FAMILY AT DOOR OF AHOM SPORTS PAVILION.

ASSAMESE BRAHMIN FAMILY.

JOYSAGAR TEMPLE.

reputation as a bloodthirsty slayer of fearsome appearance, there is another part she plays in Sakta worship. We have seen in a previous chapter how Sakta worship embraced the idea of the deity being mainly of a destructive nature, and at the same time that the processes of creation and destruction are closely linked and complementary. Creation is depicted by the sexual embrace of the god (Siva) with his Sakti, and by ritual sexual intercourse between the trained worshipper and his female partner. Death and destruction have their setting in the cremation ground.

In order to emphasize the mutual association and interplay between creation and destruction, Kali is also made to play the most prominant part in the act of creation. While still maintaining her fearsome appearance, she is the form of Shakti usually pictured in sexual embrace with Siva. And in order to give the scene its proper background, the setting is in the cremation ground. A famous hymn to Kali says " O Mother, even a dullard becomes a poet, who meditates upon thee, the naked, three-eyed creatrix of the three worlds, whose loins are beautiful with a girdle made of numbers of dead mens' arms, and who on the breast of a corpse as a bedstead in the cremation ground enjoyest Mahakala (Siva) ".

The image of Kali dancing on her husband takes a new meaning when the goddess is playing the part of creatrix. To stress the important part that she, as a woman, plays in the creation of the world, and the fact that Siva in the act of creation is entirely dependent on his Shakti, Kali takes the active superior position in her sexual union with Siva.

As a final development of the theme there is a form of Sakta worship which takes place at midnight in the cremation ground, where the worshipper, meditating on the great union of Siva and Kali, performs ritual intercourse with his sakti or female counterpart.

There is no more striking example of the way in which the Hindu mind can elaborate on a theme, and carry it inexorably through to its logical conclusion. Sakta worship among the corpses in the cremation ground is usually held up as one of the 'primitive and revolting rites' of this form of Hinduism. Revolting and macabre it may seem, but certainly not primitive. The form of worship is the product, not of dull savages, but of keen speculative minds, highly trained in religious and philosophical reasoning ; and for that reason alone is well worth a closer study.

CHAPTER V

KAMAKYAH AND THE SAKTAS

IN the account of Siva, Durga, and Kali, the importance paid in Assam (and in Bengal) to the wife or female counterpart of Siva, has been described. In fact to millions of Hindus the dual nature of the god—male and female aspects—is the guiding principle of their worship As a further development of this we see that the female aspect, or Sakti, as she is generally called, claims more and more attention, producing finally a mother goddess worshipped more or less independently of Siva. Sakti is the general term for all the female consorts of Siva, whether they be Durga, Kali, Parvati, or any of the thousand other names. The numerous followers of this particular Hindu sect are the Saktas.

To the Saktas Assam has always been a place of great importance, because certain incidents in the lives of Siva and his Sakti are associated by tradition with places in this country. By far the holiest of all these places is the great temple of Kamakyah, on Nilachal Hill, south of Gauhati, on the banks of the Brahmaputra. The well-known story which explains the origin of this holy place is as follows :—

When Siva was still a god in the making, at a time when, as a yogi of the Himalayas, he had not gained universal recognition, he was shown discourtesy by his father-in-law, Daksha. Because of this his wife, Sati, died of shame. Overcome by grief and remorse Siva wandered about the world carrying Sati's dead body on his head as penance. To put an end to this world-shaking penance, Vishnu pursued him and cut Sati's body in fifty-one pieces with his discus. Wherever part of her body fell to earth the place became sacred, but Kamakyah became the most sacred of all because it was there that the yoni (or genitalia) is said to have fallen. A finger fell at the spot where now stands the temple of Kalighat near Calcutta, and although the latter holy place is the best-known Sakta temple because of its position, Kamagiri or Kamakyah still remains one of the holiest temples to the goddess.

The temple of Kamakyah occupies a magnificent position. Situated on Nilachal Hill near the narrowest part of the Brahmaputra, it seems to guard the bottle-neck between the Assam valley and the rest of the plains of India. Behind it the Khasi and Jainta Hills rise sharply to form the south wall of the Assam Valley. As for the temple itself, it is only fair to say that, like so many other Hindu temples, it loses much of its glamour on closer inspection, and various things combine to cool the ardour of even the most enthusiastic. I visited the place for the first time at the end of March, the hottest month of the year in Gauhati. The early rains, or chota barsah, make their appearance about this time of the year in the form of occasional thunder showers, which pass over quickly giving place to brilliant sunshine.

The road up to the temple is very steep, a sort of giant staircase of boulders and great sloping stone slabs. On the way up there are several little shrines at the side of the path, one with an image of Ganesh, the elephant-headed son of Siva and Parvati. The hill-side is dotted with frangipanni or temple flower, that curious little tree which bleeds a milky sap whenever one of its blunt little branches is cracked off in the hand. No leaves have appeared yet, but it is a blaze of pale creamy flowers with a sweet cloying scent. At the top of the hill, and in the temple grounds were dozens of little Assamese girls with trays of these frangipanni flowers, white and red, which were given in return for alms.

Arriving damp and exhausted at the top of the hill, there is the additional irritation of having to remove one's shoes and cross the dirty temple yard in bare feet or stocking soles. The children are clamouring for money, and the

MIRI GIRLS FROM THE BANKS OF THE BRAHMAPUTRA.

[To face page 36]

THE AHOM PALACE OF GARGHAON.

THE AHOM SPORTS PAVILION AT RANGGHAR

temple guide appears not to understand my brand of Assamese.

Inside the dimly lit main temple are images of nine forms, or murtis, of Siva's female consort (Sakti). Strangely enough the name of Durga is not among these.* The priest said that at this time of the year the temple is very quiet, but that huge crowds collect there in June, and again later at the pujas in October. Most of the pilgrims who come from all over Assam and Bengal are women. The women usually sleep in the temple precincts for two or three days. A separate temple further along the ridge is dedicated to another form of Shakti, Bhuvaneswari, and beside it a wealthy Hindu rajah, from a small State nearby, has built a residence for himself.

The big attraction in June and July is the Ambubachi festival, or menses of the earth. This is known throughout Assam as Haht, when the earth is supposed to have its annual menstrual period. In the Assam villages this festival may last for five to seven days, after which time all articles in the house must be purified. It is also said that Brahmin widows must not walk on the earth during this period when it is considered unclean.

Europeans are apparently not allowed into the main shrine of the temple, sacred to Kamakyah, the goddess of sexual desire. The general impression of the temple and its surroundings is not stimulating ; everything is rather tawdry, unfinished, and sordid. One shudders to think of the sanitary arrangements when the hill is crowded with pilgrims. It is probable that many Europeans, who visit this place are activated by a rather vulgar curiosity, and such is the reputation of the temple, that most of them are disappointed at the absence of erotic images or spectacular rites.

As one of the great centres of Sakta worship, Kamakyah is reputed to be the scene of immoral and degrading practices. In fact the terms ' revolting ' and ' obscene '

* Kali-murti, Tara, Chinamasta, Bogola, Bubaneswari, Vairubi, Tomaboti, Matungi Komola, and Sorosi.

37

occur so often in descriptions of certain ceremonies associated with this branch of Hinduism, that it is quite obvious the writers have allowed deep-rooted prejudices to impair their judgement. An old description of one of the temples near Gauhati, called Modon Kamdeo, says : " The present objects of worship being two rude stone figures, villainously traducing the god of love and his mistress ". When moreover on further investigation we find that these ' bestial rites ' have almost certainly never been witnessed by a European, and possibly not even by non-sakta Hindus, we are quite evidently dealing with opinions based on illusion and hearsay, quite as un-scientific as the fabulous Indian rope trick.

The root cause of the trouble is that Saktism embraces and almost deifies the process of sex and reproduction, and it is this fundamental conception that most Westerners automatically shy at. But, as we have mentioned before, the idea is quite logical. Hinduism has long recognized the continual process of Creation, Preservation, and Destruction that goes on, but the Saktas have stressed the creative and destructive powers of nature, the latter being symbolised by the cremation ground, and the former by the sexual union of the male and female aspects of god, Siva and Sakti. Just as all mankind owes its existence to the sexual urge and the passionate union of male and female, in the same way the universe itself owes its creation to the embrace of Siva and Sakti. The linga and yoni, as emblems of the male and female sexual organs, have already been described, and in worshipping the yoni of the goddess at Kamakyah there is a similar recognition of the irresistable creative urge that formed the universe.

The main religious authorities of the Saktas are the sacred books called the Tantras. The religious instruction in these books takes the form of conversations between Siva and his wife Parvati. Parvati asks various questions, such as the ordinary worshipper might ask, and Siva's answers contain the main principles of Sakta worship. Much of the subject-matter is devoted to details of ritual, prayers, gestures, and repeated incantations for every occasion. The instructions are so thorough that they include such personal details as evacuating the bowels in the morning, and the ritual used when a man has union with his wife.

According to Hindu reckoning, the world at present is passing through the fourth and last phase—the Kali Yuga —a degenerate age of evil and ungodliness. Siva explains this to Parvati, and says that while men of previous ages were virtuous enough to understand and obey the most ancient Hindu scriptures, the present age has seen mankind reduced to such a sinful and degenerate state, that the ancient scriptures have lost their power, and the only hope of liberation now is to follow the instructions of Siva as laid down in the Tantras.

" Thou hast truly spoken, O Devi, of the evil ways of men, who, knowing what is for their welfare, yet, maddened by sinful desire for things which bring immediate enjoyment, are devoid of the sense of right and wrong, and desert the True Path. I speak now of that which will contribute to their liberation ", says Siva in the Mahanirvana Tantra.

In Saktic worship the union of Siva and Sakti is represented in various ways. The apposition of linga with gauri-patta (yoni) is one, or mystic diagrams (yantras) may be drawn on the ground to represent the yoni of the goddess, with sacred fire in the centre representing the seed of Siva. Another method is to dip a certain flower in red sandal paste to represent the linga, and this is inserted in another flower—Clitoria—which is shaped like the female organ. Finally there may be actual union of the male worshipper with a female, representing Sakti, usually his wife. This last method of sexual union (Maithuna) as part of the worship, is one of the elements in a ritual important to the Saktas called five elements, the Sanskrit names of all of which begin with the letter M. They are Wine, Meat, Fish, Parched Grain, and Sexual union.

The Mahanirvava Tantra says : " By partaking in accordance to the injunctions of any of the tattvas (elements) man becomes like unto Shiva. What then is the result of partaking of all the five tattvas ? " The fifth element is the one that has received the greatest condemnation from prejudiced critics, including Hindus of other sects. But the Mahanirvana Tantra lays down very strict rules about this practice ; it may only be undertaken by an advanced worshipper, who has conquered lust and gained self-control. The female partner is in most cases the worshipper's own wife, and there is little indication of the erotic orgies visualised by outsiders.

There seems little doubt that the true Sakta Hindus view this intercourse as an ecstatic union with the goddess, in a frame of mind almost unknown to the Western world. An old Assamese Mahori Babu (head man of a labour gang) once expressed it very simply. He said : " In the morning when I get up and bathe I think of God. When I eat my food I think of God, and when I have union with my wife I also think of God ".

In some parts of India, Maithuna images, showing Siva and Sakti in sexual embrace, are well known. Many can be seen in the Tantric Buddhist monasteries in Sikkim, but they are not conspicuous in Assam.

As might be imagined, some of the most intolerant and outspoken criticisms of this brand of Hinduism, which teaches sexual intercourse as part of worship, have been made by Christians. An impartial observer from another world, however, could with equal justification point to the almost morbid manner in which Christianity glorifies virginity and chastity, in the way it has exalted pure sexless love, and at the same time surrounded the essential physical functions of reproduction with an unnatural sense of shame and sin.

In this matter, more than any other, it seems difficult to keep an open mind, and acknowledge the fact that the other man also has his point of view. A great deal of harm has probably been done by libertines and debauchees masquerading as Saktas, but the general rules of conduct laid down in the Tantras are so sound and universal in

their application, that the inclusion of intercourse as part
of worship is obviously done with sincerity, and in the
belief that the worshipper gets a foretaste of that ecstasy
which accompanies final liberation, and union with the
god himself.

CHAPTER VI

SANKAR DEB
AND THE MAHAPURUSHIAS

THE Mahapurushia sect of Hindus in Assam take their name from the word Mahapurusha, meaning a perfect or super-man distinguished from all others by possessing a combination of outstanding qualities. It is a word normally used as the ideal of human beauty characterized by 32 physical signs; but it can also be applied to one of outstanding spiritual ability. The origin of the Mahapuru-shia sect goes back to the time of the great Assamese reformer, Sankar Deb.

The advent of Sankar Deb in Assam in the 16th century is usually taken as a great turning point in the religious history of that country. Previous to that time Sakta practices were prevalent, and Siva, Durga, and Kali were the dominant deities. Blood sacrifices and idol worship were in vogue, and the Brahmin priests had complete authority in all religious practices.

As a reaction towards this Sankar Deb preached a pure and simple form of Hinduism, in which he said that salvation can only be gained by devotion (Bhakti) to Vishnu, in the form of Krishna, now the sole divine being. The Tantric gods and goddesses had no part in this new scheme, and blood sacrifices and idol worship were rejected.

A similar revival of Vaishnavism at this time was taking place in Bengal under the great reformer Chaitanya; and it is probably from him that Sankar Deb gained much of his inspiration and ideas.

During Sankar Deb's time it probably appeared that the revival of Vishnuism would be complete and lasting, and that Saktism had lost its power and appeal for all time. It is true that some of his institutions, such as the simplified village prayer-house, or nam-ghar, containing only images of Krishna, have become permanent features in the religious life of the country people. His name too is still held in reverence, and celebrated every year in the Sri Sankar Deb Tithi all over Assam. But if we follow the subsequent history of the movement after Sankar Deb's death in 1569, we see that very few of his original ideas persisted, and that as time passed his extreme views of worship became toned down, and increasingly tolerant, till finally they even recognize the gods and goddesses of the Saktas. A similar failure of the Chaitanya movement in Bengal took place after the death of that even more illustrious reformer.

It is only in one religious sect that Sankar Deb's ideas have persisted with only slight modification—this is the Mahapurushia sect. After his death the followers of Sankar Deb split into two factions, the Bamun Gosains and the Mahapurushias. The former sect had already reached a compromise with general Hindu ideas; they insisted on the observance of caste, on the necessity of religious teachers being Brahmins, while they were also tolerant of idolatry, even of non-Vishnuite deities. Furthermore, they allowed the flesh of goats and ducks to be eaten.

The other sect, the Mahapurushias, under Sankar Deb's successor, Mahdab Deb, persisted in repudiating idolatry and the rule of the Brahmins. The Mahapurushias still maintain a centre at Barpeta in Kamrup, and also on Majuli Island in the Brahmaputra.

The history of the Vaishnava reform in Assam is one more striking example of the power of Hinduism to absorb and enfold even the most extreme religious views. Hinduism has proved itself tolerant of so many views, so many cults, so many gods and goddesses, that it has survived all attempts at schism. Even widely different sects find that Hinduism has something in common to offer them, something which preserves that affinity between Hindus in all parts of India.

We have seen above that Sankar Deb propounded the idea of devotion (bhakti) as being the only hope of salvation, the object of devotion being Krishna. But although this new idea seems to offer at first sight something quite opposed to the Saktas with their diversity of deities and images, his instructions are couched in such phrases as to lend themselves easily to different interpretations according to the belief of the devotee. For example, in order to convey to his followers exactly what he means by the highest type of devotion to Krishna, he says it should be like the love of Rahda, the gopi-girl, for Krishna, the cowherd. But there is surely no fundamental difference between this comparison and that of the Saktas, who say that the blissful state of the worshipper, who is finally through prayer and meditation united with Siva, is akin to the ecstasy which Parvati feels in sexual union with Siva, her husband.

It appears to be the case that the great reformers and exponents of Hindu doctrines find themselves unable to convey their ideas to their hearers without resorting to earthly comparisons ; and, after all, what could be more logical than to use the intense single-minded love of woman for man as an example on which the worshippers should base their devotion to their god.

Sankar Deb repudiated idolatry, and yet his followers soon found that the average worshipper found difficulty in continuing devotion to an abstract deity ; and as a material object on which to focus their mind seemed necessary, what more natural than an image of Krishna himself.

PLOUGHING THE PADDY FIELDS IN ASSAM.

PLOUGHING THE PADDY FIELDS IN ASSAM.

CHAUDANG GIRL TRANSPLANTING PADDY.

[To face page 45]

Chapter VII

HISTORY OF HINDUISM
IN ASSAM

THE Assam Valley might be regarded as the north-eastern limit of the great Indo-Gangetic plain of north India. It is a continuation of the incredibly flat plains of north Bengal, and is certainly not isolated from the rest of India by any great mountain barrier. All the available evidence points to the fact that the valley must have been in close contact with the culture and religion of north-east India as far back as history goes, and that there must have been a constant movement of people to and fro. The presence of a broad navigable river like the Brahmaputra must have played a big part in facilitating this intercourse.

The scenes of many events in the lives of gods and heroes of the Hindu epics and religious books, have been ascribed to places in Assam ; and the old name of the country, Kama-rupa, is taken from the incident described in the chapter on Siva, in which Kama, the God of Love, was scorched to ashes by a flash from Siva's third eye. The holy centre of Kamakyah is very old, and the presence of such a famous shrine must, in itself, have made Assam familiar, in name at least, to the rest of north-east India.

But, despite the apparent continuity, the progress of Hinduism in the Assam Valley has been very gradual, and a large number of people living in the plains are to this day animists, believing in tribal gods and spirits. In the earliest records the type and degree of Hinduism in Assam seem to have been determined by the dominant king and the length of his dynasty. If the ruling king appeared interested, the Brahmins, who were included among the early Hindu settlers, might persuade the king and the nobles to adopt Hinduism. The priests offered the additional attraction of giving the king a mythical ancestry, perhaps traceable back to Siva or Vishnu himself. Also by raising him to the Kshattriya rank they put him in the same Hindu caste as the other great rajas of north India. If the king reigned for many years, or if the country was undisturbed by war, the form of Hinduism adopted by the king would extend in time to the people.

Hiuen Tsiang, the great Chinese explorer, who spent many years travelling in India early in the 7th century, evidently considered Assam worth visiting. He was principally interested in Buddhism, and from that point of view must have been disappointed, because he found that people of Assam 'adore and sacrifice to the devas (Hindu gods) and have no faith in Buddha'.

In the following two or three hundred years there are odd records of Assam kings being ardent devotees to Siva.

The name of Assam has always been linked with that of Bengal as a stronghold of Tantric Hinduism, and many people have considered that this form of Hinduism actually originated in Assam, as a blend of Hindu beliefs with the more crude and bloodthirsty rites of the primitive hill tribes, who invaded the valley from time to time. This is an attractive theory, and appears to be supported by the fact that the religion of Sikkim and Tibet, north–west of Assam, is now recognized as a blend of Hinduism, Buddhism, and magical beliefs peculiar to the Tibetans themselves. The hill tribes round Assam, however, have always been considered low in the cultural scale. They have fairly simple animistic beliefs, and having no written language have very little to contribute to the wealth and imagination of ideas already present in Hinduism. With the exception of the little State of Manipur, in the hills between Assam and Burma, Hinduism in Assam stops abruptly at the foothills. Even the great centre of Kamakyah has had little effect on the Khasi people, who have been settled for hundreds of years in the hill districts which start immediately to the east of Gauhati. The

Khasis themselves have many peculiar animistic and magical beliefs, and one might have expected either that their views would have affected Tantric Hinduism in Assam, or that they in turn would have developed a blend of the two beliefs. There is no indication of this, and the Khasis either retain their own ideas intact, or, have become converted, in the opinion of missionaries, at least, to Christianity.

Of the various rites and practices of the Saktas, the one that seems to have been particularly popular in Assam was the blood sacrifice to the goddess. The Chutiya kings, who had their headquarters at Sadiya at the time of the Ahom invasion early in the 13th century, worshipped various forms of Kali. We have already seen how fond that goddess is of animal and human flesh, and the Chutiyas seem to have taken to heart her particular liking for human offerings. The old copper temple at Sadiya must have often been the scene of violence and bloodshed, although the victims were evidently dispatched quickly by decapitation. In most cases they were criminals condemned to death, or devout volunteers, who, like Gilbert's Nanki-Poo, were accorded attractive privileges before the sacrifice.

Up to about the 16th century most kings appear to have been Saktas, paying particular attention to Siva and Durga. At the same time, many of them, if they did not actually worship Vishnu, were at least tolerant of his followers. Bisva Singh, who came to power about 1515, one of the early Koch kings, who gave their name to Cooch Behar, rebuilt the temple of Kamakyah, and at the same time gave gifts to disciples of Vishnu. The temple was destroyed by Musselman invaders, to be rebuilt later in the same century by the great Koch king, Nar Narayan, one of the greatest kings in the history of Assam. At the time of his reign Saktism was prevalent, one hundred and forty men being sacrificed to the goddess at the opening of the new Kamakyah temple. But at the same time Nar Narayan showed a wide tolerance of all religions, including aboriginal or tribal forms. He also encouraged his great contemporary, Sankar Deb, the Vishnuite reformer, whose preaching condemned the sacrifices of the Saktas.

The same tolerance was shown by the early Ahom kings, and it is not till later that actual religious persecution between different Hindu sects occurs. The development of Hinduism among the Ahoms is particularly interesting. As we have seen, the Ahoms invaded Assam from the Upper Shan States in the early 13th century, and in a few hundred years had become rulers of the whole valley, and sufficiently strong to resist the Moslem invasion, which had swept victoriously right across North India.

The Ahom historical records, or buranjis, trace the influence of Hinduism back to the following incident. In the 14th century an Ahom king was once away from his palace fighting the Chutiyas. During his absence his elder wife, jealous of the younger one, instigated a plot to kill her. The minister, misled by the elder queen believed the younger to be guilty of some crime. As she was pregnant they did not kill her, but set her adrift on a raft in the Brahmaputra. The young queen was rescued by a Brahmin, but died giving birth to a son. The son, whose name was Sudangpha, was brought up by the Brahmin along with his own children, until, in 1397, when he had reached the age of fifteen, he was discovered by a nobleman, recognized, and put on the throne in succession to his father, who had been assassinated. The old Brahmin and his sons, who had sheltered him and brought him up, were given positions of importance, thus paving the way for Brahmin influence, and the introduction of Hindu doctrines.

One hundred years later an Ahom king, Suhungmung, also a contemporary of Sankar Deb, took a Hindu name of Swarga Narayan or Swarga Deb (Lord of Heaven), a custom permanently adopted by the Ahom rulers from that time onwards.

The influence of the Brahmins spread further, and Pratap Singh (1603–41) built temples to Siva, and also sacrificed to Kamakyah the captive son of a Musselman leader

defeated in battle. The Mahapurushia followers of Sankar
Deb had become so numerous that Pratap Singh was
persuaded by his court Brahmins to persecute them and
kill some of their Gosains or high priests.

Later in the same century (17th) Sudaipha is reported
as sacrificing to Siva, and he was followed at the end
of the century (1681–96) by the famous Godahur Singh,
who was a patron of Saktism and a persecutor of the
Mahapurushias.

He was followed in turn by Rudra Singh (1696–1714),
who appears to have had the same broad minded views
of Nar Narayan. He became an orthodox Hindu in his
old age, and while he encouraged Saktism by importing
from Bengal a famous Sakta priest, who was later put in
charge of Kamakyah temple, he also tolerated the Vishnu-
ites and stopped their persecution. Although he was partial
to the Sakta Brahmins, it is strange that one of the temples
he built—at Jaysagar—has all the stone sculpturing on the
outer walls devoted to scenes from the lives of Vishnu
and his various incarnations.

It seems fairly certain that the Ahom kings were not
intolerant of followers of Vishnu, as such, but only took
action against the Neo-Vaishnaves—as the followers of
Sankar Deb were called—when they became sufficiently
numerous to threaten the stability of the kingdom, or
sympathised too openly with the renegades and agitators
with rival claims to the throne.

There is other evidence, too, that in the history of
Hinduism in Assam the followers of Siva were never so
single minded as to worship him alone, to the exclusion
of all other gods. Vishnu, at least, has always played an
important part in their pantheon. An image found a few
years ago in Gauhati, and assigned to the 8th or the 9th century, takes the form known as Hari-Hara-Murti, the right
half of which represents Siva (Hari) and the left half Vishnu
(Hara). This type of image has been found in other parts
of India. Its introduction as the chief image in
many temples was a compromise between Sivaites and

D   49

Vaishnavites, in indicating that Siva is Vishnu and Vishnu is Siva, the two being essential components of one deity.

The temple of Neghereting, built in the reign of the Ahom king, Pratap Singh, has the principal deity, Siva, installed in the largest temple, and the other deities, Ganesh, Surya, Durga, and Vishnu, installed in smaller temples at the four corners. This worship of these five particular gods—panchadeva—is popular with a large section of Hindus in India, and the simultaneous worship of several deities figures largely in Assam at the present time.

Finally, under Rudra Singh's son and successor, Sib Singh, Hinduism became the predominant religion, and the lingering beliefs of the tribal Ahoms were rejected and fell into disuse. From that time on religious rites and ceremonies were almost entirely controlled by the Brahmins.

At the present moment most Hindus in Assam, apart from the Mahapurushias, acknowledge all the most important Hindu gods. Although primarily Saktas in that the worship of Siva and the Goddess is predominant, yet they will make prayers and offerings to Vishnu, Krishna, Ganesh, Indra, Sarasvati, and Lakshmi as well. The wealth of material in the Hindu pantheon is too attractive for them to devote all their energies and attention to one god only.

Educated Assamese, who are familiar with European ideas, often seem to think that some sort of explanation is necessary, and will say that all these deities are just so many forms of the one and only God. But it is not really necessary to offer any excuse. There is no real logical reason why worship of one god should be considered a superior form of religion to worship of many gods. Most Europeans look askance at this array of deities, but the fact that it meets the spiritual needs of millions of Hindus in a perfectly harmless way is surely a sufficient indication that the subject is certainly worth studying in more detail, and that criticism should be based on facts and not prejudice.

CHAPTER VIII

THE BIHUS

ASSAM, like Bengal and the rest of Hindu India, has many religious festivals or pujas throughout the year. Most of these, like the Durga puja and the Sarasvati puja, are held in honour of one particular god or goddess, and being purely Hindu have been introduced from outside Assam with only slight modifications. There are two festivals however which are peculiar to Assam. These are the Bihus. One of these, the Magh Bihu, has a slight religious significance, but the much greater Bahag Bihu has developed entirely along Assamese lines, and is quite unconnected with any Hindu deity.

Magh Bihu is usually known as the Assamese New Year, and falls in the month of January, usually a week or two after our own new year. At this time Assam is passing through its cool dry season. The temperature at night drops so low that the valley is shrouded with thick mist in the early morning. Near the Brahmaputra the mists may hang about so late that the sun does not appear till ten or eleven in the forenoon. These January mornings can be bitterly cold and raw, and the Assamese find it a trying time. Magh Bihu marks the turn of the season, when the sun takes a northerly course, and from that time till the rainy season the weather gets progressively warmer and drier. By this time all the rice has been harvested, and the flat 'pathar' land which was a continuous sheet of shallow water and growing rice in the rainy season, is now a great flat dry plain of pale rice stubble.

Magh Bihu is marked by its bonfires and its bathing. Because of the bonfires this festival is sometimes known as Agni-puja, after Agni the Lord of fire. Agni is one of a group of nature gods, such as Indra and Surya, whose

88380

worship was laid down in the oldest Hindu scriptures of all, the Vedas. For the last two thousand years these deities have been superseded by Vishnu and Siva, and it is only on odd occasions like this that their names are recalled.

To the boys in the village this Bihu is a sort of Guy Fawkes day. For days beforehand they have been preparing a huge bonfire or mezighar, in the form of a hut packed with straw and stubble. Early in the evening several smaller bonfires are lit, and the boys hold dancing and sporting contests. Nobody sleeps that night; the fun and feasting go on right through the hours of darkness, till finally, about three or four in the early morning the great mezighar is set alight, and is still burning when daylight comes.

The daytime is taken up with animal contests and buffalo fights. At the time of the Ahom kings this was a popular time for staging great animal contests in which buffalo, tiger, and elephant took part.

The bathing is an even more important part of Magh Bihu than the bonfires. Bathing may take place in any of the larger rivers, and in the Brahmaputra itself; but in the part of Upper Assam where I lived the favourite place was Garampani—Hot Springs—in the Nambar Forest. All who can travel to this place by car, lorry, or bullock cart do so, and by the eve of Magh Bihu there may be hundreds of people assembled there. Garampani is a little shallow pond of warm sulphur-smelling water, situated in a clearing in the heart of the Nambar forest. It is normally a silent lonely spot. The narrow road which has been winding through the thick dense forest suddenly opens into the clearing, and as suddenly the forest trees once more close in to form a solid wall of tangled green vegetation. Sometimes bands of Mikirs from the hills nearby settle down here in small thatched bashas to gather gravel from the bed of the jungle river, which near this point flows into the Dunsiri. But usually Garampani is a place of eerie silences, where tall trees cut out the morning and evening

CHAUDANG GIRLS DANCING AT BIHU FESTIVAL.

sun, and impose an unnatural gloom on the place. The forest is full of life, but it is silent stealthy life. The hooluk which livens up the foothill forests with its echoing howls, is never heard in this place. One can find the great footprints of wild elephant, and the pug marks of leopard and wild pig, but the animals themselves keep in the background. A great hornbill flying over the roof of the forest seems to complete the feeling of oppression, because as it flies its wings make a peculiar creak at each slow beat, and it needs little imagination to transform it into the rustle of some prehistoric flying reptile's leathery wings.

This then is where men and women, young and old, take to the water at the first streaks of dawn, and like thousands of devout Hindus all over India, carry out their inflexible dharma by bathing and purifying themselves for the new year.

This road that takes us to Garampani, and continues on through the forest for many miles, is worth more than passing attention. Up till recently it was the only link between the roads of Assam Valley and Manipur road which starts at the railway station of Dimapur. In the rains this forest road is quite impassible, and no car can go through direct from Assam to Manipur. But in the dry weather it will lead you along the banks of the Dunsiri river, over flimsy bamboo bridges, along narrow tracks where the car skids on the thick dust, till finally the metalled road is reached, the road that leads to Manipur and eventually to Burma.

This thick forest has not always been like this; the history books say that there must have been a well worn highway along the banks of the Dunsiri, and perhaps great open stretches of cultivated rice land, when Dimapur was the capital of the Kachari Kings. The tide of battle between them and the Ahom invaders must have flowed along this path many times. But the forest has covered it all so thoroughly now, that it might have been like this from the beginning of time. I should like to see what changes have come over this place since last I saw it. In that comparatively short interval another invasion has threatened the valley, and the sleepy little station of Dimapur, after many hundred years, has once more become a great bastion of resistance.

The Bahag Bihu is the great springtime festival of Assam. It usually falls in the middle of April—about three months after the Magh Bihu—and corresponds to the time of seed planting. The weather at this time of the year is warm and bright, with occasional heavy showers keeping the atmosphere clear. Although the countryside is still fairly dry, the Indian spring has made its appearance in the form of numerous brilliant flowering trees, Cassias, Gold Mohrs, Frangipanni and sweet smelling Mango blossom. This is the brightest and happiest of all Assam festivals, and is quite unconnected with any puja or religious worship.

Apart from the usual feasting and entertaining the Bahag Bihu is famous for its dancing and its cow-bathing. The bathing of the cows—or guru-bihu—takes place on the first day of the festival. The cows are led down to the nearest river and thoroughly washed. The old ropes are laid aside in the house, and new ones are put on the cattle. The cows heads are annointed with mustard oil (haloday) and red turmeric, and the animals are given cakes to eat. In some villages various plants are strewn on the path leading to the cowshed or gurughar, and in all cases a fire is lit in front of the shed.

For the rest of the seven days dancing and merriment go on unabated. This festival is celebrated not only by the Assamese Hindus, but also by all the numerous valley people who have not yet been drawn into the Hindu fold, such as Kacharis, Tengals, Chaudangs, Hunwals, etc. In fact it is only among these non-hindus or quasi-hindu communities that the dancing reaches its full expression. Among the Chaudangs for example there is a great deal of drinking and dancing among both sexes. Rice beer—laopani—is consumed with great relish, and sarab (distilled spirits) and bhang (hemp) are additional stimulants. I once witnessed one of these Bihu dances in a little Chaudang busti. A group of young girls, all of marriageable age, were gaily decked in their best muga silk saris, with red flowers in their hair. Large groups of ten, twenty to thirty, may take part. Some of the girls beat time with 'tawkas', large clapping instruments made from a thick bamboo stem split along part of its length. The dancing girls usually form a circle facing inwards, and move their feet in time to the rhythmic beat of the tawka—shaking their bodies at the same time. The dance is really a sort of syncopated shuffle, the girls keeping their hands on their hips at first, but now and then raising them in the air with rhythmic movements. During all this time their faces remain expressionless, and their eyes are cast on the ground. Finally they give a last rippling shake of their shapely bodies, and the dance ceases abruptly.

Among these people the marriageable girls dance in public, and at night are joined by the young men of the village who have their own form of dance. The young men's dance is usually more violent and energetic than that of the girls, and they are well fortified with lao-pani. One of the youths beats rapid time on a drum or dhul, using his hand and fingers ; others make a hideous noise with clashing cymbals or tala. Another plays tunelessly on a pipe (pepper), which takes the form of a flute attached to a hollow buffalo horn. Others again beat time with two wooden bamboo sticks (lakri). The dancing itself is not particularly picturesque.

As the night goes on and the beer circulates, the tempo increases, and nobody pays much attention when a boy and girl slip away from the dancers into the darkness. Many an affair is started or brought to a climax at the Bihu dancing.

The dancing customs seem to vary quite a lot depending on the race or locality. In general however among the higher class Ahoms and Kalitas the dancing of marriageable girls takes place in private, or inside a house or shed, and the men are not allowed to watch it. This is probably a restriction imposed by Hinduism, and is well in keeping with Hindu ideas of womanly modesty and behaviour. In Bihu days there are always plenty of men dancing in such villages, but only the very young girls (chookries) are allowed with the boys. In most Ahom and Kalita villages there is no drinking of lao-pani such as is common among the Chaudangs and Chutyias, but 'bhang' is quite a common mild stimulant.

The bhang (Indian hemp) is bought in shops, mixed with milk and sugar, boiled, and then drunk. Taken like this, and only at Bihu times, it is said to have no harmful effect on the village boys, and it certainly brightens up the festivities.

My Bengali babu tells me that a corresponding festival in Eastern Bengal at this time of the year is the 'Chaitra Sankranta', which differs from the Bahag Bihu in that there is no village dancing. The only dancing on that festival is done by trained troupes of travelling performers.

CHAPTER IX

SOME RELIGIOUS FESTIVALS AND BELIEFS IN AN AHOM VILLAGE

BESIDES the main Hindu puja days which are well known all over Assam, there are many festivals peculiar to the villages. Some of these festivals, prominent in one village, seem to be unknown in another. The educated Hindus in town appear to take little interest in these obscure pujas, and remain rather obtuse about their own beliefs. It is certainly the case that some of the festivals described here, which are well known in a little Ahom village on the banks of one of the side loops, or Sutis, of the Brahmaputra, are unknown to many educated Hindus in a town only 15 miles away.

The first of these is in honour of the goddess in various forms. It is called the Bisawari puja in honour of the seven sisters (saht baheen) or seven mothers, who are saktis or female counterparts of the main gods. The names of the seven goddesses together with the names of the gods from whom they are derived, are as follows :

Durga or Maheswari (Siva)
Saraswati or Brahmini (Brahma)
Kaumari (Karttikiya, son of Siva)
Indrani (Indra)
Lakshmi or Vaishnavi (Vishnu)
Varahi (Varaha, and avatar of Vishnu)
Narasimhi (Narasimha, another avatar of Vishnu)

The festival, which is unknown to the Brahmins and Kalitas, is held without any officiating Brahmins. All the village people subscribe some money towards it. The date is finally fixed by the old men of the village, and usually falls about the beginning of June. The two outstanding items are the construction of a large raft or house boat, and the sacrifice of goats, ducks, and pigeons. The raft is made by the village boys from banana stems. At about midday, all the people in the village wend their way to the namghar or village prayer house. Songs are sung, and puja performed, several goats, ducks and pigeons being sacrificed. The goat's head is struck off with one stroke of the dao, the blood is poured onto the raft, and the carcase eaten later at the evening feast. On the raft are placed little lamps (Bhatti), flowers, and other offerings, as well as a considerable amount of money, up to one hundred rupees (about £7 10s. 0d.) depending on the size of the village. Two live ducks and two live pigeons are also placed on the raft with enough food to last them for two or three days. The lamps are lit and the raft is moored in the stream.

In the evening there is a feast at which the sacrificed animals are eaten. It is also said that anyone interfering with the raft or its offerings will be punished by death, and that was certainly the fate of one Miri man, whose dead body was found on the river bank the day after he had stolen some coins from the raft.

An even lesser known festival takes the form of a religious dance. This seems to be the only occasion when high caste Ahom and Kalita men and women dance to-gether. It is usually performed by the young men and their wives. In some villages this dance is held regularly once a year, but there is no fixed date or festival for it. A considerable amount of money is required for food, clothes, offerings, ornaments, gold and silver etc., and as a result very poor people may be debarred from performing this rite.

The dance takes place at night, starting after midnight. It is noteworthy that it is held in secret, nobody else being allowed to witness it. About twenty men and their wives go into a large room or house, and close all the doors and windows. The women wear a special costume con-sisting of a short skirt, and a piece of cloth wound round the breast. They wear numerous ornaments of gold and silver, necklaces, and special broad Assamese bangles extending half way up the arm. Their hair is loosened, and on their heads some wear a brass vessel (kahi) and several lighted lamps (bhatti). The men wear only short dhotis or loincloths, with no shirt.

The dance and song go on for two or three hours till early in the morning when they have a feast. A raft of banana trees has been constructed on the river. Numerous offerings are placed on this, then it is floated off and sunk, after which the dancers return home.

The village people are familiar with all the main Hindu gods and their consorts, particularly Durga in her various forms. Siva is also known as Hodakia, and Vishnu by the names of Isor (Iswar) and Hori (Hari). Besides these there are various local gods and sprites; such as the Apeswaris or Apsaras who are the delightful female hostesses associated with Swarga, the heavenly court of Indra. Also Juleswaris or water goddesses such as we might expect in a part of the country interlaced with rivers, bheels and sutis. Some gods, like Krishna, are supposed to reside in trees, but there are also special tree gods which seem to have no Hindu counterpart; these are the Dangooria or great ones, who reside in a large tree called 'Kodom gos'. I heard of one villager who unknowingly or unthinkingly cut down some trees from a kodom gos grove, to make a dugout. The particular Dangooria of this grove became displeased, and the villager's youngest daughter suddenly became ill with a high fever. Someone finally diagnosed the cause; a special puja was quickly arranged, offerings of fruit were made, several bhattis were lighted, and ducks and pigeons sacrificed to the 'great ones'. The Dangooria was appeased and the child rapidly recovered.

All unusual natural phenomena are also attributed to different gods. Assam is very subject to earthquakes, slight tremors are not infrequent, and most grown-ups have heard or experienced severe shocks which knock down houses. The usual Hindu explanation of this is that it is due to one of the four elephants, which support the corners of the earth, shaking its head. The Assamese say that the earth is supported on the shoulders of the god Nag. He is supposed to support the earth for a year on each shoulder, and normally seems to manage the job with a steady hand. But when there is a great deal of evil and wickedness in this world—alas only too common in this degenerate fourth age or Kali yuga—the earth becomes heavy; oppressed with the weight Nag shakes with anger, and an earthquake results. There were several sharp earthquake shocks in Upper Assam at the end of January 1941, and this was held to be another indication, if any more was needed, of the sin and wickedness of the world.

Early in 1942 there was an eclipse of the sun visible in this part of the world; this was interpreted as Indra, the Lord of Heaven, going into consultation with the other gods. The hill tribes round Assam usually attribute this to some animal, such as a tiger (Naga tribes) or a frog (Khasis) trying to swallow the sun or the moon, but the Ahom belief is evidently dictated by Hinduism.

Coming at such times these phenomena were treated very seriously, and it was strange that another unusual thing was seen in 1938. One day I saw a perfect circular rainbow caused by the almost vertical sun shining through a thin vaporous layer of cloud. A little Nepali man with me looked at this and said 'A very bad sign sir, it means there is going to be a big war'. Little did he think at that time that not only would the war materialise, but that it would be brought almost to his doorstep.

CHAUDANG GIRLS DANCING AT BIHU FESTIVAL.

COURTYARD OF ASSAMESE TOWN HOUSE WITH SHRINE.

[To face page 61]

CHAPTER X

SOME ASSAMESE MARRIAGE CUSTOMS

IN Assam the influence of Hinduism in moulding the lives
and beliefs of the people is very striking, and nowhere
more so than in its effects on marriage customs and ceremonies. Just as we find in the valley all gradations of
religious belief from animistic to orthodox Hinduism, so
also there occurs a wide range of marriage customs,
determined principally by the degree of conversion to
Hindu beliefs. Roughly speaking the higher we go in
the Hindu scale, the more elaborate becomes the cere-
monial, until we find among the Brahmins marriage very
similar to that of the rest of Hindu India.

As far as the Assamese Brahmins are concerned, the
determining factor in the choice of partner is the horoscope.
The Hindus throughout their history have shown abundant
evidence that if a subject is worth any attention at all it
is worth investigating well. Once a belief has become
established, nimble brains get to work classifying, elabor-
ating and enlarging every theme to a volume of commen-
tary, in a manner bewildering to the Western mind. And
so it is with horoscopes, where the general plan, compre-
hensible to most educated Brahmins, has been built up to
form a system which needs a specialist to interpret.

Every Hindu who can afford it, has his horoscope cast
at an early age. This is based entirely on the hour, day
and month of birth. On what constellations are in the
ascendent at the time of birth; what the phases of the moon
are, and so on. All this information is built up into an
elaborate chart, originally made out on bark, but now on
paper. From this, astrologers with the necessary training
can work out all details of the person's temperament,
weakness, proportion of Brahmin and Kshatriya blood,

lucky and unlucky days, days favourable for marriage, and even the approximate time of death.

My Assamese Brahmin friend admits with a smile that marriage is almost entirely a matter of mathematics. Personal inclination or mutual attraction play very little part in making a marriage contract. The attitude of some Hindus who have had a scientific training is rather interesting. To a European they will perhaps admit that the whole system is based on superstition alone, but they find it difficult to resist its fascination, and will quote numerous instances where incidents in people's lives were foretold by their horoscope. As a basis for lifelong partnership it is possibly no more illogical than the unaccountable fancies and infatuations that lead so many Europeans irresistibly to the altar. In fact the Hindu system has the advantage that both parties are convinced that if their horoscopes tally favourably, it is quite impossible for the marriage to be a complete failure.

When a Brahmin, Kayastha, or high class Kalita wishes to arrange a marriage for his son, he looks round for a likely family of good social position like his own. If this family has a daughter of suitable age and appearance, enquiries are set going by means of an intermediary. He approaches the second family, and in course of conversation remarks ' Your daughter Phuleswari will soon be preparing for marriage ; Have you made any plans about her future husband ? ' If an arrangement has already been made, or if the girl's father is thinking of making negotiations elsewhere, the subject is dropped. But if nothing has been fixed already, the mediator suggests that Suryakumar Goswami's son Ram seems a likely lad and is worth considering. If the girl's parents have any objection to this boy or to his family's social status, the negotiations break off without offence on either side. If however the girl's parents are not averse to the suggestion, they reply that it might be worth considering, not committing themselves in any way. Enquiries are then set going on both sides to find out as much about the boy and girl as possible.

All information or casual talk directly or indirectly given by brothers, friends or acquaintances of the boy is collected, and it is unlikely that any unpleasant characteristics or diseases can remain concealed after this enquiry. Finally, if all is satisfactory up to this point, an exchange of horoscopes is arranged, and a pundit is called in to draw up a complete horoscope of the suggested union. It may transpire that in the event of such a marriage, the girl may become a widow at an early age, or the marriage will be barren, or the boy die of fever before he is thirty. Any such clause would be sufficient to cancel the proposed contract immediately. It is unlikely that the two horoscopes will tally in all points, and if six clauses out of nine coincide, that is usually regarded as sufficient to ensure a successful marriage.

Once the horoscopes are found to tally on most points, an attempt is made to introduce the two young people. In many cases the boy is not very keen on seeing the girl himself, and the mission is entrusted to someone else, who brings back an account of the girl's appearance and accomplishments. Appearance and health are the main factors, because once the final agreement has been reached the girl can be trained and educated according to her future husband's ideas. Provided the horoscopes agree in most points, it is unlikely for the boy to object to the agreement, and it is unusual for mathematics not to win the day.

Among the Brahmins this marriage, or rather betrothal, takes place very early, when the girls are eleven, twelve, or thirteen, seldom later than fourteen. But the actual wedding ceremony and consummation do not take place till after puberty. In this the Brahmins differ from most other Assamese, where the boys and girls are fully grown and developed before they marry.

Once a Brahmin is betrothed she is considered married in so far as she becomes a widow if her future husband dies. A young girl may therefore become a widow without even having seen her betrothed. As a Brahmin widow she is not allowed to marry again, and may be condemned to spinsterhood while still a virgin. The problem of the virgin widow is one that effects the whole of India. Fortunately in many places the custom is becoming less rigid, and the outlook of the Brahmin widow is not quite so hopeless as it used to be. In this respect the Assamese Brahmins are less progressive than those of the neighbouring Bengal, where widow re-marriage is not unusual, and is on the increase.

Among most high caste Assamese Hindus the wedding ceremony is preceded by a purification ceremony, which takes place on the nights immediately preceding the wedding day; for three, five, or seven nights according to the wish of the parties concerned. On the same night the bride's party and the bridegroom's party go and collect holy water from some large tank, not necessarily from the same tank. The water brought back is used for anointing the bride and the bridegroom, after which new garments are put on.

The collecting of the holy water takes place at night or in the early morning, and probably for that reason is a much less common sight than the wedding procession itself. The first one I saw, about nine o'clock on a dark June night, consisted of a small party of Assamese women together with young girls (chookries) from the busti. The procession was headed by a villager with a hurricane lamp. As they walk the women sing in unison, led by an old woman (buree). With a high pitched piping voice she chants :

" Ram Krishna ghar ako juagi."

Then all the other women's voices join in together :

" Ram Krishna ghar ako juagi."

As the silent man heading the procession passes along the road, his swinging lamp flickers on the white saris of the women, giving them the appearance of a ghostly procession of angels in white raiment. And the sound of the young childish voices approaching, passing, and dying away again,

MECH GIRLS FROM THE NORTH BANK OF THE BRAHMAPUTRA.

[To face page 64]

THE OLD KARACH FORT AT DWAINTE

gives the ensuing silence a chill and sadness strangely at variance with the wedding rejoicings.

There are numerous songs that can be sung, or rather chanted, on such occasions. They are mostly of religious nature and call on God in the name of Ram Krishna (Ram and Krishna being forms of Vishnu that appeared on earth in human form) to bless the boy and girl. The procession described above was that of the bride's party. The women who bring water to purify the bridegroom proceed in much the same way, but may have different songs, such as :

"Ram Krishna meg-he borochiso
li-ri-ki li-ri-ki borochun ahiso."

Although most Ahoms of good family are now completely Hinduised in their religious views, they have certain wedding customs which mark them off sharply from the Brahmins, Kayasthas, and high caste Kalitas. This is probably one of the reasons why Assamese always draw a distinction between Hindus and Ahoms, drawing attention to the fact that the Ahom Hindus still retain a few tribal customs, and are only comparatively recent converts compared with other Hindus.

In the case of Brahmins, Kalitas and other orthodox Hindus, a Brahmin officiates at the wedding, and he lights the sacred fire (home) which is made of mango sticks. The bride and bridegroom pour ghee (clarified butter) on to the sacred fire, and there is an exchange of 'pan' leaves between the two.

In the Ahom wedding ceremony, however, it is not necessary to have a Brahmin officiating, and although many do have one, he does not light the sacred fire, but merely talks with the boy and girl repeating instructions and prayers. Furthermore there is no exchange of pan leaves between the bride and bridegroom, and they do not pour ghee on the fire.

When the wedding is arranged, the bride's father besides giving a substantial dowry, gives also a bed, clothes for two years, and all cooking utensils. The bridegroom's father provides house and ground, golden ornaments such as bangles, necklaces, and earings for the girl, and also the wedding dress. Other expenses of the wedding such as food, presents, and priest, are a joint concern.

For the three days before the wedding, while the bride is being purified as described above, she does not eat her usual food, but confines herself to milk and banana.

Like the usual Hindu custom the bridegroom's procession goes to the bride's father's house where the wedding ceremony is held. If the distance is not too great they go on elephant back.

There are some Ahom families who claim direct descent from the Ahom kings, and they take the name Raj Kumar. They differ from the usual Ahom custom in that the bride goes to the bridegroom's house to be married.

Before the boy arrives at the girl's house on the wedding day, the bride is bathed and attended by village women. She puts on her meghela and new clothes, and her hair is anointed with oil and carefully combed, while the women sing appropriate songs.

At the wedding ceremony bride and bridegroom wear garlands of flowers such as ' dogor phul ' and ' tulasi phul ', and at the culmination of the ceremony the girl places the flowers on the boy's head, and he places the flowers on the girl's shoulders. After the ceremony the bride and bridegroom are showered with rice, as they depart for their new home, or to the boy's father's house. The bride may go alone or with a girl friend from the village, and for the first three nights in the new house the young married couple sleep separately, the bride either alone or with her village friend. During these three days the couple are only allowed to talk with each other. After the third night the village girl departs, the young couple greet each other and declare their undying affection, after which the marriage is consummated. After a week the bride returns to her mother's house with her husband, and they stay there for a few days before returning to their own house.

Among the Chaudangs who live near Jorhat and Sibsagar there is no true marriage ceremony. Most of this tribe are beyond the Hindu pale as they may eat pig's flesh and drink rice beer or lao-pani. But, as described earlier on, some of the well-to-do Chaudangs are adopting more and more Hindu customs.

Normally among the Chaudangs there is a fairly free and easy system of love. A boy and girl may carry on an affair before marriage, and there is a great deal of surreptitious love-making. In many cases a boy may acquire a wife by paying a certain sum to her father. In other instances if the girl does not return the constant attentions of an ardent suitor, he collects several of his friends together and they raid the girl's house ; sticks and daos may be used if the girl's brothers and kinsfolk put up a resistance ; eventually the girl may be taken away to a distant busti. If the boy pays the usual bride price to the girl's father, all may end happily, otherwise the case may find its way to the law courts.

CHAPTER XI

SOME CUSTOMS RELATING TO BIRTH, MATURITY, AND DEATH

THE average Assamese villager is particularly desirous of having a large family of sons who can help him with the farm work when they grow up, and provide for him in his old age. On the other hand a large family of daughters is a definite liability, as the expense of marrying them off is so enormous that he is likely to be in debt for the rest of his life. The girls themselves are brought up with the idea firmly implanted in their minds that for them marriage and child-bearing is the summum bonum, and nobody's lot could be more hopeless or unfortunate than that of the barren woman or the childless widow.

The young wife who has not yet conceived will do everything in her power to induce fertility. The Ayurvedic medical books have innumerable recipes to ensure fertility, and the old 'burees' of the village itself have accumulated a store of traditional knowledge to overcome barrenness. The childless woman will offer up prayers and sacrifices to Durga, and may even undertake a visit to the temple of Kamakyah in Gauhati.

Similarly, the men folk, although tending to lay the blame for a childless marriage on the wife, will also consult the local hakim about measures they may take to ensure and prolong virility. How important the whole subject is to the Hindu may be gauged by the space devoted in the daily papers to patent medicines for overcoming impotence, and prolonging virility and manhood. They may be in the form of medicines, charms, or talismans, and are immensely popular. Even the highly educated, serious-minded Hindus consider that the study of aphrodisiacs and stimulants well worth attention ; and the classical

Hindu treatise on Love—the Kamasutra—devoted many pages to medicinal preparations and recipes.

When a woman becomes pregnant she ceases to have any connection with her husband from four months before the child is expected. It is a common belief in the village that as a pregnant woman's time approaches it is possible to tell the sex of the unborn child. If the woman remains plump, healthy, and good looking, the child she is carrying will almost certainly be a girl. But if the woman becomes weak, emaciated, and ugly-looking, it will almost certainly be a boy.

While many of the Brahmins call in the services of a professional midwife or 'dhai' of low class to assist in the birth of the child, the Ahom custom is different. An old experienced Ahom woman of the village is the only one to assist at childbirth. The pregnant woman squats on a heap of clothes on the floor, while the old woman holds her shoulders from behind. This custom also differs from that of the tea-garden coolies where several women crowd round the expectant mother and make a fearful clamour during labour.

After the baby is born the umbilical cord is cut with a sliver of bamboo, and the baby is washed with warm water. The afterbirth is buried in the compound.

There seems to be no taboo or active prejudice against twins, although they are not particularly welcome because the mother has to feed and provide for two children at a time instead of one. The village people believe that there is a strong bond between twins, and that they are really halves of one and the same individual. As an instance of this, there were two twin girls we shall call Leela and Beela. These girls shared the same feeling and emotions ; when one was sad so was the other ; illness or dysentery in one was invariably shared by the other. Even the simple calls of nature were said to effect them simultaneously. The monthly periods of the girls coincided exactly, and the girls felt ill at ease when out of each other's sight even for a short time.

When a young girl of twelve or thirteen has her first menstrual flow she is considered unclean and is confined to the house for nine days. During that time she must not look at or talk to men, even the menfolk of her own family. During that time she also has frequent baths and changes of clothes. After the nine days are over the women of the village celebrate the occasion with a dance in private and the singing of songs celebrating the 'pohila jewan' or first menses. After that time the only regulation which attends menstruation is that the girl must bathe very early every morning; she may go out of doors during her period, and she must not prepare any food. If married she sleeps apart from her husband in a separate bed.

When it comes to funeral customs, the Assamese customs again reflect the influence of Hindu beliefs. When a man is dying he is usually carried out of the house, as it is considered a bad augury for the household if he dies indoors. Should this actually happen, the house is abandoned after the man's death, and nobody will ever live under the same roof again.

All Assamese Hindus burn their dead in a funeral pyre. The body is first washed, anointed with oil, and finally new clothes and a clean winding sheet are put on. After the body is consumed in the flames, the ashes are buried, and over the mound a small shelter is erected.

When returning from a funeral ceremony, after burning the dead body, it is a common custom for the mourners to purify themselves by putting in their mouths and on their feet some leaves of 'titaphul,' a plant with thick dark-green leaves like laurel bushes, with a bitter taste. This is supposed to act as an antidote against any poisonous vapours or evil odours.

While the Brahmins burn all dead bodies, including those of children and still-born infants, the Ahoms have a different custom. With them, all dead infants and children up to the age of nine or ten are buried, while any one of a later age has the body burnt.

At a fixed interval after the burning of the body the

family hold a feast to which are invited relatives, friends, and all who assisted before or after the death. The feast is held in some open place, or within the courtyard if it is a large house.

Among the Brahmins and Kayasthas it is held twelve days after the funeral, and among other castes it is usually after thirty days. A priest officiates at the feast and is given presents of food and clothes for his services. It is customary also to ask a very old man, whose death can not be very far off, to this feast; he is the first to partake of any food because it is said that the person who starts the feast will be the first to die.

Chapter XII

VILLAGE LIFE

The impressions that one gets of Assam as a whole depend mainly on which part of the country one has settled in. The man living in Shillong or the Naga Hills will think of Assam as a hilly country with delightful cool weather. In most of the valley itself, however, the dominant impression is that of a vast flat plain, ringed a great distance away by a faint line of hills. In the plain patches of pathar (cultivated land) are mingled with tangled jungle and forest, great swamps and bheels, and trim orderly tea gardens. There are places in Upper Assam where one can drive hundreds of miles without meeting any great variation of rice field and busti (village), bamboo bari and tea garden, bheel and jungle. The plain too seems to run smoothly to the very foot of the hills, and end abruptly there in such precipitous slopes and thick impenetrable forest that even the roads seem discouraged, and peter out in forest tracks and narrow Naga paths.

Strangely enough, throughout most of the valley one is hardly aware of the great Brahmaputra winding its way across the plain. The country is so flat that for miles along its banks the land is a succession of swamps, side loops or sutis, and strange rivers which flatten out so much towards their mouths that their waters seem too weary to cover the last lap, and lie about in sluggish indecision.

In the dry weather the Brahmaputra sinks back into its sandy bed, and leaves behind a confusing wilderness of sand banks and lagoons which change from year to year. The river steamers probe their way up a marked course, through narrow shoals which may be sand banks by the following week.

But in the rains the Brahmaputra becomes a great

72

turbulent menacing flood, spilling over its banks, thrusting back the waters of its tributaries till they in turn spill over onto the flat rice land, and turning the flat country on either bank into such a succession of swamps and bheels that great tracts of country have become unsuitable for villages and cultivation.

Away from the big river we find typical valley scenery of flat rice fields and little busties. Only a few of these busties merit the name village as we understand it. They are mostly little groups of houses, separated perhaps by only a few hundred yards from the next group. They cluster together on ground slightly raised above the level of the rice fields, and are surrounded by clusters of bamboo trees, banana, mango, jackfruit, paw-paw and so on. The rainy season which floods all the rice fields to a depth of a few inches, turns these busties into little islands or oases, which are only reached along the narrow little alis, or low earth bunds which separate the rice plots from each other.

Although the land appears so flat—we may be six to seven hundred miles inland but only 250 feet above sea level—full use has been made of the slightest gradient, and the innumerable rice plots, or ketts, are connected in such a way that rain water alone can keep them flooded for four or five months. If there is too much water in the ketts after heavy rain, an opening can be made in the low bund by removing a few sods of earth; the surplus water can then be run into a slightly lower kett, and so on till a natural stream or jan is reached, which carries the storm water to the large rivers.

There appear to be no borderlines between one villager's ketts and another; no fences or boundary marks; and yet each villager knows his plots from all others, and preserves the undefined boundaries. The understanding does not always remain so tacit and perfect, and real or imagined extension of one man's mutty, or ground, on to that of his neighbour's leads perhaps to blows and a long expensive law suit.

In the rice fields the cycle of changes each year affects

the appearance of the whole landscape. In the dry cold weather the whole flat rice plain has been harvested, and the ground is hard and dry. Over this plain herds of humped cattle now roam, browsing on the rice stubble. They are looked after by little chowkras (boys) and brought back every night to the shelter of the cow house. This regular return of the cattle is associated with the Assamese word for evening, goduli, which might be freely translated as 'cow-coming-home-time.'

With the coming of the early rains in April and May, little rice nurseries are fenced off with interlaced bamboo splints, and the rice seed is sown densely over the small area. The rice ketts are now beginning to collect water, and by May or June, when the ground is covered to the depth of a few inches with water, the ploughing is carried out. The feet of the oxen churn up the soft ground and convert it into a quagmire, through which the ploughman wades. The fields are usually ploughed three or four times, a separate name sometimes being given to each ploughing. The heavy plough work is usually done by the village men, but many families hire the labour from the low class Doms or Kaibortas. No Brahmin man will touch a plough, and even the poorest of that caste will get somebody else to do his ploughing.

After ploughing, the churned up mud is smoothed over by a man standing on a flat wooden board pulled by bullocks or buffaloes. By this time the isolated rice nurseries have produced a dense lawn of the brightest green rice seedlings. Towards the end of June and in July the rice seedlings are transplanted from the nurseries to the muddy bed of the kett. While the bundles of seedling are carried from the nurseries to the ketts by men, the actual transplanting is done entirely by women. This is a strenuous job, and coincides with one of the hottest and most oppressive times of the year.

On the day when planting starts there is usually a feast in the evening, and another one at the end of the last day of planting. The Chaudangs have a puja both at the

sowing of the seed in the nursery, and later at the transplanting. The pujas are often held under a banyan tree,
and are followed by dances, after which—among the
Chaudangs at least—many of the village lads sleep with
their girl friends.

During July all stages of transplanting can be seen,
from recently ploughed fields to those dotted with little
seedlings. At this time too tall bamboo poles are often
erected near the fields, with a little flag at the top. This
is in honour of Lakshmi, the Goddess of Prosperity, and
the Protector of Padi. As Lakshmi is particularly worshipped by women, whose job it is to plant the rice, the flag
may have a twofold origin.

By September the whole rice plain is a magnificent
stretch of bright green well-grown rice, with the water
still shimmering round its roots. Later the water dries
up, and by the time the rice is ready for harvesting late in
December, the ground is firm and dry. The harvest home
in January is followed quickly by the Bahag Bihu festival.

Assam has a very regular wet south-west monsoon
period, and suffers less from droughts than any other part
of North India. As we have noticed, most of the rice
fields on the plain rely entirely on rain water to fill them,
and there is no need to carry irrigation water to the plots
from rivers or high ground. The water table is so high
during the rainy months that flooded fields dry up very
slowly, even in those odd periods of several days drought
which are liable to occur in the middle of the rainy season.
The Assamese farmer is thus fortunately placed, with an
assured crop, and little chance of drought or famine.
However, the old people in most villages remember odd
years of, if not actual drought, at least unusually low
rainfall, or an abnormally late monsoon. In one little
Ahom village I have talked to an old woman who took
part in a rain-making ceremony when she was a young girl.

Two good young girls are chosen from the village
children. Each one takes a frog, which they can find
easily in the dry weather hiding inside the house. A

purohit (village priest) is called in, and the two frogs are put through a marriage ceremony on the usual Hindu lines. Red marks are put on the heads of the frogs, ornaments are hung round their necks, and marriage songs are sung by the village people. Finally the frogs are bathed by the two young girls, and the people can now look forward with confidence to rain within seven days.

A striking feature of the Assam Valley are its roads. In most of this flat swampy country the rainy season would put a complete end to communications if it were not for the fact that the roads are embanked, and run for miles raised above the level of the surrounding country. In this stoneless alluvial soil there is no stone that can be broken down for road metal, and it all has to be brought from long distances. Many of these roads owe their existence to the Ahom kings, who fully realized the importance of all-weather communications, and who had huge forces of conscript labour at their disposal. The main artery connecting one end of the valley with the other is the grand trunk road, over four hundred miles long, running from Lakhipur in the south to the Lohit at Sadiya. As the road runs for mile after mile along the top of a great bund or causeway, one realizes the immense amount of labour that must have gone into their making.

Great lengths of this road are shaded with trees planted along either side, in the narrow grass fringe that separates the road from the jungle, swamp, or rice field. In the old days of slow leisurely transport this shady avenue was a cool sanctuary in the hot hours of the day. But now the herds of cattle which graze along the roadside, and rest anywhere on the cool shaded road, are a continued source of annoyance to swift moving traffic. Tea planters running up to Shillong for local leave will vie with each other in recounting the number of times these infuriating cattle brought their cars to a standstill; and a few impatient drivers will tell their total bag for the day in cattle forcibly butted out of the way, or impetuous goats which rushed madly to their deaths under the wheels of the car.

Away from the main roads there are innumerable minor roads. Many of these have distinctive names, such as the Dhodar Ali or Lazy Man's road, built in the time of King Godapani by labour which had volunteered for any other work but road making. Other familiar ones are the Kamaraband Ali, the Kharakatia Ali, and the Naga Ali, and so on. Only those who have had to tackle these roads in the rainy season can appreciate how terrible they can be.

In contrast to the thickly populated parts of the valley with rice fields and innumerable busties, the country just south of Sibsagar offers an interesting contrast. This is one of the few places in Assam rich in historical relics. This was the capital of the late Ahom kings who ruled up till the last century, and it is here that they built the great palaces of Garghaon and Rangpur, the sports pavilion at Rangghar, and several temples at the edge of enormous tanks. The great fresh water tanks, entirely excavated by hand, still remain the finest in Assam.

The temples and ruined palaces appear at first sight to be genuine antiques, the relics of some ancient civilisation or remote dynasty, with their crumbling walls eloquent testimony to the passing of centuries. It is with something akin to horror that one hears that they are little over two hundred years old. If such stout and solid brick buildings can disintigrate in that short time, little wonder that there is scarcely a trace in the country of the great towns and palaces of former days.

Up till the end of the seventeenth century the palaces and buildings of the Ahom kings were built mainly of wood, with occasional supporting pillars and gate posts of stone. The houses of the people were made entirely of bamboo, wood, mud, and thatch much the same as the average busti house of the present time. But Rudra Singh who lived at the beginning of the eighteenth century decided that brick would be a stronger and more lasting material for his important buildings. There was no one in Assam who knew sufficient about brickwork for this purpose, so a skilled mason from Koch Bihar was persuaded to come to Sibsagar and undertake the work. The mason, once he had got the work on a strong footing, was not allowed to leave the country alive, as it was suspected that he had accumulated rather too much ' information useful to the enemy.'

The great palace at Rangpur which he built is now a complete ruin, a historical record disintigrating before our eyes. A broad staircase overgrown with moss, leading to a level grassy lawn surrounded by a ruin wall, is all that is left of the great audience hall, which, with its massive pillars and timbered roof must have been in those days an imposing setting for state functions. In a better state of preservation are the king's private chapel, the women's quarters, and in the basement, the great vaulted rooms which housed the king's bodyguard and the dungeons and torture chambers where so many of the king's enemies met a brutal death.

Rumour has it that a secret underground passage runs from Rangpur to the older palace of Garghaon many miles away. A tangle of vegetation has completely covered the royal bathing pools, and is sweeping in from all sides to cover the walls and the floors as the vanguard of decay and disintegration. The seeds of the pipal tree lodging in crevices in the walls give rise to robust plants and shrubs, which in the course of growth split the masonry asunder. The heavy rain and the hot humid climate continue the work of destruction, which is further accelerated by periodic earthquake shocks. Now the palace presents a scene of desolation, accentuated by the emptiness of the surrounding country which is almost devoid of villages. Great herds of cattle roam over the grassy plain which was once the royal deer park and hunting ground.

The sports pavilion at Rangghar is still well preserved and a delightful cool place even on the stickiest and sultriest July days. It was built exactly 200 years ago, in 1745, under Rudra Singh's second son, Pramata Singh.

The great tank and the temple of Joysagar date back

to the time of Rangpur. Joysagar tank is another example of the lavish scale on which the Ahom kings made use of their conscript labour. Unlike the famous tanks of Ceylon, which were formed by building massive bunds across the mouths of valleys and damming back the water to form vast lakes for irrigating dry land, the Assam tanks were all excavated by hand on flat country to a depth sufficient to ensure an abundance of water right through the dry season. It is possible that these four huge tanks, Sibsagar, Joysagar, Rudrasagar, and Gaurisagar, were not all built for pure utility, as any one tank could supply abundant water for the whole district, and as there is always plenty of rain in the long monsoon season to render irrigation quite unnecessary.

As the Ahom kings became more Hinduised they would become more familiar with the idea of achieving spiritual merit by good works. For example the Mahanirvana Tantra says " Those who give away tanks and so forth for the comfort of all beings are washed of all sins, and having attained the blissful region of Brahma reside there a hundred years for each drop of water which they contain." Corresponding merit could be gained by building brick temples, bridges, and causeways, all of which figure prominently in the public works of the late Ahom kings.

Recently, some of these derelict tanks have been used by an enterprising young Assamese Brahmin to develop a fresh water fishery scheme. By a system of canals and culverts water can be collected from the extensive Rupahi Bheel, and the fish, trapped by bamboo fences, are driven up the Gaurisagar where they are netted or stranded.

Associated with the name of Joysagar is one of the best known stories of Assam, that of Joymati, the Ahom princess who died to save her husband. How much of this story is based on fact is difficult to say; it is not usually included in the history books on the country, but nevertheless to most Assamese Joymati remains the outstanding female figure in history, and the embodiment of wifely virtue and devotion.

Joymati was the wife of Godapani who later took the name of Godahur Singh, and was the first of a series of outstandingly strong Ahom kings who ruled in the latter part of the 17th century and the earlier part of the 18th. Godapani spent his youth in an atmosphere of treachery and bloodshed, of weak vicious kings and plotting nobles, and of torture and unbelievable cruelty. In 1675 his father, Gobar, had been on the throne barely a month when he was assassinated, and his predecessor in turn had been murdered after a brief reign of 21 days. Gobar's successor was also assassinated, and he was succeeded by a boy rajah, 'Lora Rajah.' While some favoured this unsatisfactory monarch, others were plotting to bring Godapani to the throne. At this time Godapani was hiding in the house of a Garo or Naga woman, called Dalimi, dressed like a peasant and working in the fields like the other villagers. Meanwhile the boy rajah, suspecting that his own position was not too secure, decided, like many of his predecessors, that a very sound line for him to take would be for him to kill off all possible rival claimants to the throne starting with Godapani. As Godapani could not be found his wife Joymati was secured, and although she was the daughter of a noble family, Bargohain, she was treated with great brutality. Handed over to the cold-blooded hereditary executioners, the Chaudangs, she was tortured publicly at the 'jering pathar' or punishment ground, in order to force from her the whereabouts of her husband's hiding place. The torturing went on for several days, the princess being beaten with 'surat pat,' a poisonous plant with intense, nettle-like stings. Then she was flogged and branded, and finally succumbed without giving away the secret.

Godapani's share in the story is not clear, and the common version suggests that Dalimi's charms made his stay in the peaceful little Garo or Naga village not entirely unpleasant. However, it is Joymati who is the central figure, and her faithfulness and devotion right to the end is in keeping with Hindu ideas of the perfect wife and

[*To face page* 80]

mother. Her noble deed is still celebrated in the annual
Joymati Utsev which is held on the banks of Joysagar,
and attended by large numbers of Assamese men and
women, including prominent figures in Assam society.

With the help of one of the great nobles Lora Rajah
was ousted from the throne, and later murdered. When
Godapani came to the throne in 1681 there had been seven
kings in the previous eleven years, none of whom had
died a natural death.

By Joymati's self sacrifice she is often known as the
Assamese Sati, by resemblance to the self-immolation of
Siva's wife described elsewhere in this book. The story
forms the basis of many Assamese stories and plays, and
was the subject of the first talking film in Assamese, with
an all Assam cast.

In the domestic life of the Assamese Hindus, whether
in town or country, one of the most striking features is
the communal household. When a man's sons marry,
instead of moving off to another village or setting up
house of their own, they tend to remain as part of the
father's household, even living under the same roof.

Suppose for instance three brothers marry, their wives
will all come and live in the same household, and all the
children will be brought up together as one family. In
Assam one is frequently amazed at the number of children
coming out of a single house, and it is natural to make
the mistake that they are the numerous progeny of one
man and his wife.

In the town the joint family often live in a single large
house of many rooms, but in the villages it is more usual
for additional small bamboo houses to be added on as the
family increases.

In the joint house, the old mother while she is alive
usually holds a position of authority, and if she chooses
can sometimes make life rather unpleasant for her
daughters-in-law. When she dies, the wife of the eldest
brother becomes the head of the household, and is respons-
ible among other things for the cooking. The wife of

the second brother looks after the children, while the youngest brother's wife keeps the house clean and tidy.

Sometimes, of course, one of the brothers may decide to set up house of his own, or may have to move to another part of the country according to his job. But Hindu families are usually large enough to ensure that there are sufficient numbers of brothers to keep the communal household going.

In most cases each male member of the household is earning money either as a clerk, or by sale of farm produce, or by some other means. In such cases the resources are pooled. When the family contains a black sheep who cannot or will not earn money, he is still entitled to his share of the joint earnings, and can live a pleasant parasitic life supported by his brothers.

In the country such a household is almost entirely self-supporting. For weaving cloth and making clothes, country silk and cotton are used. The cotton or kapok comes from inside the enormous seed pods of the simil tree, which with its great buttressed roots is one of the most impressive of the Assamese trees. About the end of April and the beginning of May the simil seed pods burst open and release the fine down which floats through the air like thistle-down. The simil cotton is used for stuffing pillows and mattresses.

Assam has long been famous for its country silks, of which there are three kinds. The Mohammedans cultivate a small silkworm, something like the European mulberry silkworm, which produces 'pat' silk; while the Assamese cultivate the famous 'muga' and 'eri' silkworms.

The Muga worm is fed almost entirely on a small bush called 'phutaka,' which grows commonly on waste ground, and resembles a small rhododendron bush. The Eri on the other hand can feed on three different plants, the commonest of which is the 'eri pat' or castor oil plant. In country roads one may frequently see village men and girls carrying huge bundles of these eripat leaves to the villages from places where the plant grows profusely.

The job of looking after the silkworms and weaving the silk is done by the old women of the village. These light brown silks are used for the ' meghela ' (skirt) and ' riha ' by the Assamese women, and also for shirt and cloak for the men.

Rice cultivation is another activity of the joint household, although in many of the higher class Assamese families the strenuous transplanting is done by hired labour. Some of the larger households have rice mills, but the usual method of husking is by the dekhi, a heavy piece of wood supported horizontally in see-saw fashion, so that pressing one end with the foot raises the other heavy end with its wooden pestle, which is then allowed to fall, pounding the rice in a small depression in the ground. Pounding rice with the dekhi is well known to be tiring strenuous work, and it is the object of many a village tale and proverb.

A conspicuous feature of every village are the bamboo baris, great clumps of tall willowy bamboos, like tufts of giant grass. They supply material for building houses, fences, cowsheds, bullock carts, and innumerable other articles of every day use, as well as providing a greatly esteemed delicacy, young bamboo shoots. In fact the tall clumps of bamboo are as marked a feature of the Assam Valley as the coconut and Palmyra palms of South India and Ceylon.

Round the yard of village houses one may see sheaves of ' til ' (sesamum) laid out in the sun. The grain is used for making Assam bread, which consists of til and rice mixed together with ' ghur ' (molasses). The village people also prepare from the ' til ' a cool reddish hair oil which is very popular in the hot weather.

Many Assamese bustis grow jute or ' mora pat ' which is retted in water, the fibres extracted and cleaned, and sold to the kyas or Marwari middlemen. Various other food plants are grown such as ' dhal ' (pulse), mustard, Indian corn, vegetables, and less commonly, sugar cane. There are also the various fruit trees, the shady mango which fills the air with sweet-scented blossom in April and May ; the Lichi so popular with the flying foxes ; Banana trees like bedraggled windmills ; jungle plum trees ; jack fruit, pineapples and many others.

The Assamese Hindus are not orthodox in their diet, eating the flesh of goat and ducks. Each household usually possesses a lot of livestock, buffalo, cattle, goats, ducks and pigeons. The cattle are often given names, as they are in this country, such as ' Horu Boga ' (Little White One), or ' Kola Mok ' (Black face), and are among the most valued possessions of the villagers. In fact the position of a man in the village community can often be gauged by the number of cattle he owns.

In the daily life of the villagers washing and bathing take a prominent place, and most of them bathe at least three times a day. On getting up in the morning the first thing is to offer up a small prayer, and in the larger households there is usually a special small room or covered-in place for this purpose. Then follow the calls of nature, which in the country as opposed to the town usually means a visit to the jungle near a river or stream. In fact the all-embracing Shastras, or books of religious instruction, do not omit this simple and necessary function, giving full details as to exactly where and when the bowels should be evacuated.

This is followed by the first bathe in the river, men and women bathing in different parts or at different times. The married women have only a short bath, but the unmarried girls stay in the water much longer. The bathing is carried out with the customary modesty of the Hindu ; with the women the sari is worn in the water and there is no unnecessary exposure of the bodies. The men likewise never strip completely, but always retain at least a thin strip of cotton round the loins.

After the bathe, about seven in the morning, there is the first meal with tea and puree. After that the usual round of domestic duties for the women, and about ten they begin to prepare the midday meal. At midday the young girls bathe in the river again, and this is followed by the midday meal, which consists of vegetables, ' bhat ' (cooked rice), potatoes, sometimes goat meat or duck. Later in the afternoon there is another light meal with tea and puree, and about five or six, before sundown, there is another bathe, brief for the married women, but prolonged for an hour or so in the case of the young village girls, swimmimg, diving, and playing. The men and boys have their afternoon bathe about an hour earlier. The men never bathe with the women, or watch them from the bank. In the evening about seven or eight, there is a final meal and the villagers retire to bed about ten.

These details about feeding and bathing naturally vary from place to place, depending on the status of the Hindu householder. The higher class Assamese Hindus have several changes of garment for different occasions. After bathing, the women of the house always change into a red sari, a red blouse, and a red chowder when cooking food, and these garments are changed after the meal. Before starting a meal it is often customary to mutter a short prayer or grace, and among the illiterate country people the first morsel of food is raised to the forehead before being eaten as a silent offering to the gods. Meals are usually taken seated on a low stool, and the type of dish used varies largely with the means of the family. Well-to-do people have special vessels raised to a convenient level on a high stand. These utensils are expensive, and the village people may simply use a brass bowl or ' kahi.' The poorer families, and also garden coolies and hill people feed off plantain leaves.

In most Hindu families the woman of the house dines along with her husband, but it is also quite common for the wife to wait till her husband has finished before she starts. In most Hindu homes dining is a very private affair, and there is often a special room for the use of the family only, into which only the most intimate friends and relations are allowed. In his own home even the Brahmin man relaxes, removing his shirt and stripping to the waist at meal time, assuming a guise unfamiliar and slightly disconcerting to the European who knows him only in his official or babu capacity.

In many ways life in the country village is similar to that of villages in other parts of the world, being made up of the hundred and one little duties that constitute the day's work. The women tend to gather round the dekhi or the cooking pot at the back of the house, and discuss the latest births, marriages, sickness or death. The village lads have lots to keep them busy with the crops and the farmstead, tending the cattle and livestock, repairs to house and fences, cutting bamboos or firewood, fishing in the river, and also at intervals going into town with the bullock gari, a day's work in itself.

The village girls help with the housework, bring water from the tank or river, wash the clothes, fish in the river and bheels with their triangular ' jakai ' nets, and look after the numerous children attached to the household. Hindu influence shows itself in many ways outside religion. Many of the boys are named after Hindu gods and heroes such as Ram (Rama), Harikrishna, Deveswar; the termination -iswar means god, and -iswari means goddess. The -iswari termination is very common among the girls, such as Phuleswari (Goddess of flowers), Pramateswari (Goddess of strength), Loteswari (Goddess of the lota, a religious vessel), and Paneswari (Goddess of water). Other girls names are taken from famous female characters in Hindu mythology, such as Sita and Savitri; and others are those of Assamese queens such as Rupahi and Deopadi.

In the village houses, corresponding to our Family Bible, is a copy of the Ramayana, by far the most popular and widely read Hindu classic. Assamese children very early become familiar with the various stories from this great epic, whether told by word of mouth, or read to them by some elder brother, or a literate relation. The story of Ram (Rama) and his battle with the demon king Ravan (Ravanna); the faithful Hanuman and his host of monkeys; Sita, the ideal of wifely virtue; Lakshman, the faithful companion, and Kaikeyi the plotting queen, are all characters as familiar to the Assamese Hindus as Red-Riding-Hood, or Jack-in-the-Beanstalk to us. Like the Bible, an oath taken on the Ramayana cannot be broken.

Stories from the Hindu classics and stories of the gods are also popular subjects for village theatricals, where at night by the light of a flaring hurricane lamp one can see the old favourite, Krishna and the Gopi girls, or the Kirat Arjuna. The young boys and men of the village will also present plays based on stories from Assamese history, the female parts being played by the young boys. Once these dramatic shows start, all sense of time is lost, and when we slip silently away about midnight the village audience are still following intently every word and gesture.

Besides beliefs in minor deities, some of which have been described in a separate section, there are numerous superstitions about witchcraft, the evil eye, and various animals. In many of the village plots one can see an inverted pot stuck on the top of a pole to avert the evil eye, and many of the troubles and ailments afflicting a household are attributed to the malign influence of some human being. One hears of an old woman in the village who is slowly wasting away because someone has put a spell on her, but when she is finally persuaded to visit the hospital the evil spell turns out to be an attack of dysentery which is quickly cleared up by a course of 'bezi doi,' needle medicine, or injections.

There are many fantastic stories attached to animals, and it is rather natural that snakes take a prominent place in their imagination. The villager cutting a path through thick scrub or jungle will mutter 'Garuda, Garuda' invoking the aid of Vishnu's attendant bird, the enemy of snakes. The name of 'King of the Snakes' goes, not to the King Cobra or Hamadryad, but to the Banded Krait, one of the most poisonous and at the same time most sluggish snakes in Assam. Its habit of lying about paths near habitations is well known, and is said to be due to the fact that the female cannot become pregnant till a man has stepped across its body. It is also said to eat other snakes, though this is more characteristic of the Hamadryad.

Another snake is said to be able to fly or glide from tree to tree, the tree on which it finally settles eventually withers and dies.

In the jungle the red dog is supposed to have very acrid pungent urine. When hunting its prey it runs round the animal blinding and stupifying it with its urine, till the animal is too weak and dazed to resist the final onslaught.

Another animal, possibly the civet cat, is said to defaecate always in the same pit which it makes early in life. When the pit is full the animal dies.

The Assamese regard elephants as forms of Ganesh (Gonees in Assamese), the elephant-headed son of Siva and Parvati, and on this account it receives great respect. It is to Ganesh that the mahouts salaam before mounting, and custom also says that women may never ride on the back of a male elephant as this would be an insult to the god. Elephants are reputed to understand everything that is said about them, and never forgive anyone who speaks evil. They are also very sensitive to the behaviour of their mahouts; if a mahout sleeps with his wife he must purify himself by washing and putting on fresh clothes before mounting the elephant. If the mahout disregards this, forgets to change his dirty clothes, or sleeps with some other woman, the elephant will most assuredly throw him off when he tries to mount. The mahouts are supposed to possess special powers which give them control over their elephants, and to make use of Jadoo—magic—and bewitching songs.

Another belief is that elephants are afraid of going into large rivers because of a small spiny fish which can get into the elephant's feet and kill it. When the elephant approaches such a river it salaams it several times by raising its trunk.

Most of the rice fields along the foothills and near the forests have little raised bamboo platforms or machaans which are used in the harvest season as watch towers for the villagers, who beat empty kerosene tins and drums to keep the elephants away from the crops.

Sometimes an old rogue elephant from being a nuisance actually becomes a danger to people themselves. A few years ago one such pugli hathi or mad elephant caused great damage and panic over a wide area of country near the Brahmaputra. It knocked down houses, chased people and actually ate them when it got the chance. After a month of terror and confusion it was finally shot by the agent of one of the riverside ghats, and eaten in turn by the Miris. The Assamese say that when a man is chased by such an elephant he is not safe even when he climbs a tree; if the tree is a small one the elephant will push it down, otherwise it will fill its mouth with water and squirt it at the base of the tree like a high pressure hose, washing the earth away from the roots and weakening the anchorage till finally the tree can be pushed over.

CHAPTER XIII

TOWN LIFE

LIKE India in general, most of the Assamese people live in the country, and the number who settle in the few small towns is only a very small fraction of the whole. But like everywhere else towns play a noticeable part in the lives of the village people; with their big markets and bazaars, their shops and their stores, they attract the country people from all round, as they bring in their produce to be sold, to spend their money on some gay trinkets, a silk sari from Gauhati, a new hurricane lamp made in Hong Kong, a brass bowl from Muslim Kumars, some stomach medicine from the pharmacy, cotton shirts, perhaps a brace of goats, or a cheap Japanese bicycle.

The town has plenty of amenities unknown to the little villages; and a visit to a sick relative in the big hospital, or attending a case at the law court, is a good excuse for spending a day in town and seeing the sights.

These towns are perfect examples of haphazard, unplanned, growth; imposing houses of wealthy Marwari merchants or Assamese Government officials stand cheek by jowl with decrepit hovels and hideous corrugated iron-roofed shacks. Little attempt is made to beautify the compounds, and many are disfigured by rank vegetation and broken bamboo fences, and perhaps even ornamented by the rusting carcase of some ancient motor car, long dead but still unburied.

The few European compounds with their trim lawns and Hibiscus hedges are admired but not copied by the Indian people. On the other hand parts of the town have an orderly beauty which owes much to the natural lush greenery of the country. In the centre of the town there may be a fine expanse of green park or maidan, surrounded by gold mohur and cassias. Or it may be a large rectangular tank with water lilies dotted on the surface, an unspoilt relic of the Ahom kings.

As we might expect also the town is more cosmopolitan than the country. In one street one may see a remarkable variety of races. There are tall bearded Punjabis with short trousers and loose shirt outside. Bengali Musslemen; Marwaris, the great trading and money-lending community. Kabulis, Nepalis, Khasis and a host of others. In the cool dry weather many of the hill people come to town from the mountains encircling the Brahmaputra Valley. Particularly conspicuous by their scanty garments are droves of Nagas. In the same morning one may have visits from travelling box-wallahs from countries as far apart as Manipur and Kashmir, and one is offered a tempting display of Yarkand wool rugs, silk and camel hair shawls, tussore silk from Manipur, gaily coloured native cloth, to say nothing of innumerable weapons and curios, brass bowls from Manipur, Nepali kukris, Tibetan copper plates, and the usual seemingly inexhaustible supply of carved and inlaid ivory junk.

From the Himalayan side of the valley a few long-haired, disreputable looking Bhutias may enter the valley, their speciality being patent medicines, lucky charms, tiger claws and whiskers, bear fat, and perhaps even some rare Rhinoceros horn, and any other unusual ingredient guaranteed to cure piles, eliminate hernias, cure leprosy, or increase virility.

Patent medicines are in enormously wide demand, and as there is no restriction on sale or advertisement, there is no limit to the fantastic and impossible claims made by the makers. Advertisements for lightning cure remedies occupy prominent places in such popular daily papers as the *Amrita Bazaar Patrika* and the *Assam Tribune*. Many of them are concerned with curing venereal disease or increasing virility. Perhaps in this prolific country, where fertility and child bearing are part of one's religion, the Assamese Hindus are unusually sensitive about their reproductive powers ; the women in deadly fear of the stigma of sterility, and the men making desperate attempts to stave off the evil day when impotence finally overtakes them.

It is in the towns naturally that we would expect change and progress to be most obvious. One of those urban features which is having an increasing influence on the lives and ideas of the people, both town and country, is the cinema or ' bioscope ' as it is usually called. While the European community have their own regular American and English film shows in the planters' clubs, the town cinema shows are mainly confined to Indian pictures, in Hindustani, Bengali, or occasionally Assamese. These Indian-made pictures cover a wide range of subjects. Some are action pictures full of thrills and adventure, the Indian equivalent of the old Wild West type. Others are historic, and others again—and they are probably the most popular—deal with the ordinary lives of the Hindu people in India, and with ' dharma ' or religious duty or conscience. The popular heroine of these pictures is no glamour girl or heart breaker, but one who shows all the womanly and wifely virtues, love and fidelity, gentleness and compassion. Among the most popular of the female stars are Devika Rani, Pramilla, and Sadhona Bose, and although their pictures are spoken in Hindustani or Bengali, the average Assamese seems to have little difficulty in following the story or conversation.

The introduction of the bioscope and the ' talkie ghar ' probably means more to the Assamese woman than to the man. Seated in the purdah balcony of the picture house, and concealed from the eyes of the men folk, these women who spend so much of their lives behind the scenes, can identify themselves with the female characters in the film, and follow the actions and scenes as intently as if it were their own lives that were being depicted. These pictures have little appeal to the European because of the difficulty in following the rapid conversation in an alien tongue, but occasionally there is one with a more universal appeal

where actions speak louder than words. Such a one was
'Jadoo Nagar,' or the Magic City, in which full use was
made of all the arts of trick photography. There was the
wicked rajah who used magic to work his evil designs, but
who like Wells' 'Man Who Could Work Miracles,' failed
to win the affection of the girl he desired. There was the
incredibly active hero whose favourite trick was to hold at
bay with his sword, not one, but a whole circle of armed
adversaries. There was the ever popular funny man and
his partner, who was repeatedly exposed to the indignity
of being transformed by 'jadoo' into a woman and back
again. A lot of the back chat is lost by not knowing the
language, but from their actions and the effect on the
audience, there is little doubt that the Indian comedian is
an expert in his own line. Finally, when it looks as if Evil
will be triumphant there is a flash of lightning and Vishnu
appears in a blaze of glory, to the chagrin of the rajah of
Jadoo Nagar, and to the joy of the united lovers, and all
ends happily.

In recent years purely Assamese films have been appear-
ing, and although the standard of acting and photography
can hardly compare with the products of the great Indian
film companies, they are immensely popular. The first of
these, 'Jaymati,' dealt with a famous Assamese story
which is described elsewhere in this book. A later one,
'Indra Maloti' had a modern setting, while the most
recent one, on the eve of war, was 'Monomati.' This
picture was from a historical novel based on the third
Burmese invasion of Assam, and in it the Burmese leader,
Mingimaha, is finally murdered by a captive Assamese
girl, Padumi.

To the Westerner the Assamese town, like most towns
in north India, seems to be entirely peopled by males.
Whatever improvements there have been in the emancipa-
tion of Indian women and in the gradual easing of purdah
restrictions, the vast majority of Hindu women prefer to
remain behind the scenes in their own houses and court-
yards. It is only occasionally that they appear in the open

streets in any numbers, such as on the festival days described elsewhere in the book. This absence of women from the streets appears even more striking when compared with the large hill towns such as Shillong and Imphal, where the great bazaars are almost entirely peopled by Khasia and Manipuri women, who dominate the scene entirely. But in a town of the plains it is only rarely that one is granted a glimpse of these elusive high-caste Hindu women and girls. On odd occasions a troop of these girls used to pass my house on their way home from school or college. The young girls of marriageable age are delightful creatures; slim, with perfect carriage that no westerner could hope to emulate; dressed in graceful saris, and all, almost without exception, having the most perfect glossy hair, black ' like a swarm of bees,' and usually of remarkable length, sometimes so long that when unplaited it reaches the ground. Rain or shine these girls always have their umbrellas up like parasols, but strangely enough even the older girls are nearly always barefoot. These girls being unmarried always have the head and hair uncovered. As students too they have dispensed with the little red mark on the forehead, which in Bengal is put on when the girl is first betrothed, perhaps at the age of seven or eight, but in Assam is not usually put on till the girl reaches puberty. Later, when these girls marry, an additional red line is drawn along the centre parting of the hair, and the sari or chowder (shawl) is pulled up over the back of the head, and fixed in position with gold ornaments. These girls keep their hair in a beautiful glossy black condition by liberal use of cockila tel (cocoanut oil), narikal tel (Palm oil), til tel (oil of sesame) and arrange their hair in one or two long plaits. In the married women the hair is usually tied up in a bun.

The Chaudang girls one may see in the town on festival days also arrange their hair in enormous buns, the centre of the bun being made of a ball of wool round which their own hair is wound.

The women of the hill state of Manipur have not such

a wealth of hair as the plains women, and they try to improve their appearance by tying to their own hair chignons made from other women's hair.

A fairly recent introduction to the town is the cycle gharry or tricycle rickshaw ; with the cyclist in front, and room for two on the hooded seat behind, this is a particularly suitable form of transport for the level town roads. By pulling a blind down in front the occupants can remain completely concealed, while still able to see out through a small spy hole in the screen. As can be imagined this is very popular with purdah or semi-purdah women, and offers a speedier and more up to date version of the old palki or palanquin. The lighter ladies of the town also find it useful, and some of the Khasia courtesans can be seen plying regularly between their homes on the outskirts of the town, and the centre where their favoured customer of the moment, possibly the Punjabi manager of the local cinema, is living. Although they are really hill people these Khasis deserve more than passing mention because of the extent to which they invade the towns of the valley. The women, or Khasianis as they are called in the plains, are brought up in a country—the Khasi hills—where matriarchy predominates, and where the men are relegated to a position, as one Khasi expressed it, of mere 'breeding bulls.' The women are by nature and upbringing entirely mercenary and promiscuous. Endowed with striking good looks they are the most successful courtesans in the valley, with no distinction of race, colour, or creed.

From time to time musical shows and plays appear in town. It may be a school dramatic club acting a play written by a local Assamese, or it may be a varied musical show of school talent, or again it may be a full band of skilled musicians from Gauhati or Bengal. Few shows are complete without one or more of the classic dances from great Hindu epics or lives of the gods and heroes, such as Krishna and the Gopis, the Kirat Arjuna—a combat between Siva disguised as a Kirata or mountaineer, and the great prince Arjuna—and the dance of Siva. There is nothing amateurish about these performances, and although the significance of the various mudras or gestures which tell so much of the story, is lost on the European, many of the performers seem to get so absorbed in their theme that they actually appear to live the part of the god or hero they are impersonating.

In many Hindu homes the young girls are encouraged to learn to play some musical instrument such as the sitar (4-stringed instrument), tanpura (3 strings), or tokari (1 string); and many of them while still young reach a stage of proficiency when they can play with confidence before an audience. In a more highly trained band one can see all these stringed instruments played together, as well as others such as esraj (stringed instrument with bow), tobla (small drums, the right one of the pair being made of wood, and the left one of earthenware), and dolsotranga (a xylophone of glasses struck with sticks). Sitting cross legged in front of the platform one of the players may suddenly break into an Assamese song, in that peculiar tremulous plaintive throaty way so typical of India. The musical shows are patronised almost entirely by Assamese and Bengalis, the women in the front seats and the men behind. But although they are completely Indian shows, the odd European who shows any interest finds himself welcomed with perfect courtesy, and far from being an intruder is made to feel as if he is really the guest of honour.